# MY LIFE AFTER DEATH

*Overcoming and Learning to Live*

# MY LIFE AFTER DEATH

*Overcoming and Learning to Live*

ELIZABETH
PATTERSON

MY LIFE AFTER DEATH
Overcoming and Learning to Live
By Elizabeth Patterson

First Edition
Copyright © 2025 by Elizabeth Patterson

Published by
EANP Independent Consults

For permission requests, contact

Hardcover: 978-1-960299-74-1
Paperback: 978-1-960299-75-8

# Contents

# Foreword

by Lucy Quist, Author and Convenor
of *The Bold New Normal*

Elizabeth is one of the most remarkable women I have ever met. It's easy to speak of ambition. But to persist, to act on it relentlessly, that is the true test. What happens, though, when your ambition is to serve others, even when faced with seemingly insurmountable odds? How do you reclaim your life and rise to your fullest potential after it's been upended?

Elizabeth's story begins with a life moving perfectly on course until, in the blink of an eye, everything changed. Through her life-altering accident, gruelling recovery, and unshakable focus on possibility, she invites us on a journey of grit and discovery. Her resilience fuels a passion not just to survive, but to thrive.

Life's challenges, especially those that alter us irrevocably, can make it easy to believe we've lost the chance to live fully. Yet Elizabeth defies this. She challenges us to embrace every facet of life with arms wide open, even the joy of bringing new life into the world amid her own transformation.

Hers is the story of a straddler: a woman who navigates the complexities of both Western and emerging-world realities. Perhaps this duality is what sharpens her vision; a passion to see women everywhere emerge as the butterflies they were meant to be.

From my first encounter with her years ago to this day, Elizabeth remains the same confident, compassionate, and tireless force I've always admired.

As you turn these pages, take your time. Pause. Reflect. Return to the passages that speak to you. May her story ignite in you the same fire to live—fully, fiercely, and without limits.

# Prologue

LIFE HAS A WAY OF REWRITING OUR STORIES when we least expect it. One moment, I was a vibrant teenager with dreams as vast as the sky, the next I was fighting for my life in a hospital bed, my future suddenly uncertain. This is not a story of tragedy, though tragedy plays its part. It's a tale of resilience, redefining possibilities, and finding purpose in the face of adversity.

In the pages that follow, you'll journey with me from the bustling streets of Ghana to the hallowed halls of American universities, from moments of deep despair to triumphant victories. You'll witness how a life-altering accident became the catalyst for a mission that would touch the lives of countless girls in Africa.

This memoir challenges the very notion of disability. It asks us to reconsider our preconceptions about limitations and potential. Through my experiences—as a student, an advocate, a professional, a mother—I invite you to see the world through a different lens. A lens that focuses not on what's lost, but on what can be gained when we refuse to be defined by others' expectations.

BUT THIS IS MORE THAN JUST MY STORY. It's a testament to the power of education, the strength of the human spirit, and the ripple effect that one person's determination can have on an entire community. It's about the girls whose lives have been transformed, the barriers that have been broken, and the dreams that have taken flight.

As you turn these pages, prepare to be challenged, inspired, and perhaps even changed. For in the end, this is not just a story about overcoming disability. It's about discovering ability—in ourselves and in others—where we least expect to find it.

Welcome to my journey of redefinition. Welcome to a world where limitations are just illusions waiting to be shattered.

# CHAPTER 1

# A Miracle Birth

I AM WRITING THIS BOOK on the 21st anniversary of the day that changed my life forever. It gives me pause for reflection, not just because I survived a life-altering car crash and a bad thing happened to me, but because of all the absolutely incredible things that have happened to me–things that I have accomplished and done in the past 21 years that I would never have thought possible after I came out of my coma and faced my new life with anxiety and trepidation.

Fast-forward almost two decades. As I cradled my newborn son in my arms on that November day in 2018, I couldn't help but reflect on the incredible journey that had brought me to this moment. It seemed like only yesterday that the idea of bearing a child and giving birth naturally had felt like an impossible dream, a mountain too high to climb. But here I was, holding the greatest blessing of my life, a living testament to the indomitable spirit that resides within us all.

Throughout my pregnancy, I kept this precious secret close to my heart, sharing it only with a trusted few—Andy, mother, and sister. I had asked those who saw me to refrain from capturing my image, knowing that the sight of a visibly pregnant woman with disabilities was a rarity in our world. The usual celebrations that come with pregnancy—the photoshoots, the social media announcements, the gender reveal parties—had no place in my journey. Instead, I held onto a quiet strength and an unwavering belief that carried me through each day.

When the moment finally arrived, and I held my son in my arms, my mother sat beside me, her phone in hand. With my blessing, she began sharing the news with our family, their voices echoing joy and congratulations through the phone. But amidst the happiness, a question lingered: "Why did you keep it from us?"

Upon hearing of his grandson's birth, even my father had asked about the nature of my delivery. "Did they cut you?" he asked, blunt and to the point, assuming that a cesarean section had been necessary because of my physical challenges. His words, unintentionally hurtful, served as a reminder of the assumptions that often accompany those who live with disabilities.

In the days that followed, as I shared pictures of my son with loved ones, the distance between us seemed to grow. Few made the effort to visit us in the hospital, the airbnb we stayed in for two weeks, or the White Plains apartment we eventually moved into, the physical separation reflecting the emotional distance that had formed. But as I looked into my son's eyes, I realized that the true miracle was not in the perceptions of others but in the unbreakable bond that we shared.

At that moment, I understood that my story was not one of limitations but of boundless love and unwavering determination. And though the road ahead may be uncertain, I knew that with my son by my side, I could face any obstacle that came our way. In this book, I hope you will learn that in the face of adversity, the human spirit has the power to rise above, reminding us repeatedly that there is no "dis" in disability—only the limitless potential for resilience and renewal.

As I lay in the hospital bed, my newborn son nestled in my arms, I couldn't help but feel a twinge of sadness amidst the joy. Andy, my boyfriend, father of my children, and life partner was still in Ghana, was unable to share in this precious moment, and even though my mother was by my side, the absence of my other loved ones was palpable. And for reasons I had yet to understand, Agatha, my sister, even though she didn't live far away, only showed up to visit me at the hospital a couple of days later. She had her then-boyfriend (now husband) in tow, who we barely knew, and I somehow got the impression my baby boy and I were just another tick on her list of Saturday chores she had to get done. My father did not show up at all, supposedly because he didn't want to run into my mother, who had become his ex.

When my aunts called to congratulate me, their happiness seemed to carry a hint of superficiality. While they expressed their joy at my ability to give birth, I couldn't shake the feeling that their words were tinged with surprise, as if the very idea of me conceiving a child was a marvel. One of my aunts even questioned my mother about my fertility, as if the notion of me being with someone and creating life was an anomaly.

When people meet me, they often can't see past my physical disabilities. The paralysis on my left side, the limp in my walk—these are the things that seem to define me in their eyes. But they fail to understand that these are merely external manifestations of the challenges I've faced. They don't define who I am as a person nor limit my capacity to love, dream, and create life.

I remember once, someone had the audacity to ask me if I was capable of having sex. It was a question that caught me off guard, not even because it was so personal, but because of the sheer ignorance it conveyed. With a mix of frustration and patience, I explained that my injury was in my brain, not in my reproductive system. The fact that I had a child was a testament to my ability to engage in the most natural of human experiences.

It saddens me to think that these misperceptions and prejudices clouded what should have been the most joyous moment of my life—the birth of my son. Instead of basking in the pure love and happiness that a new life brings, I grappled with the weight of society's narrow-mindedness.

But even in the face of these challenges, I refuse to let them dim the light my son has brought into my world. For he is a reminder that life's greatest gifts often come in the most unexpected packages and that the human spirit has an incredible capacity to overcome, love, and thrive, no matter what obstacles may lie in our path.

I had gone to New York for routine doctors' visits and checkups and only found out while I was there that I was pregnant. My mother had not wanted me to go back to Ghana to have the baby because, as much as I love my country, they are still in the dark ages when it comes to disability rights. They would have surely viewed me as a high-risk pregnancy and insisted I have a C-section, which I did not want. So, we decided to spend my pregnancy term in New York so my son could be born there. We still had a house in Queens, where we had lived for many years, but it was rented out at the time. This meant we were jumping around from Airbnb to Airbnb throughout my pregnancy. If my son grows up with wanderlust, I will only have myself to blame.

As the first telltale signs of labor became known, I

found myself in an Airbnb in Queens which had become our home away from home apartment, just me and my ever-composed mother. The moment my water broke, a cocktail of excitement and sheer terror started coursing through my veins. We called the hospital, hoping for a step-by-step guide on how to navigate this uncharted territory. They advised me to count the minutes between contractions as if I were timing a particularly intense game of charades.

With each passing contraction, my panic reached new heights. I pleaded with my mother to hurry and get us to the hospital before my son decided to make his grand entrance right there on the living room floor. But in a moment of pure maternal priorities, she insisted on applying her makeup, determined to look her best for her grandson's first moment. I wasn't sure if she was planning an Instagram or Facebook debut for her and her grandson, but that was definitely not on my agenda.

I, on the other hand, had no time for such glamorous pursuits. I threw on a pair of sweatpants and a t-shirt, channeling my inner Olympic sprinter as I made my way down the stairs of our Airbnb, silently cursing the inventor of stairs with each step.

As the rain pounded against the windshield, my mother drove us through the streets of Queens, to the hospital, our beacon of hope in the early morning. I couldn't help but wonder if my son had already inherited my flair for dramatic timing. When we finally burst through the hospital doors, I hurried through the paperwork like a contestant on a game show. My body was already telling me to push, which I did without even thinking. And just like that, a mere 15 minutes after we entered the hospital, Andrews Kofi Nyarko Nii Larte Lartey, who we call Drew for obvious reasons, made his grand debut, ready for his close-up.

As I held him in my arms, I couldn't help but marvel at the incredible strength of the human body, the sheer determination that allows us to bring new life into the world, even when we feel like we're barely holding it together ourselves.

As births go, Drew's was like a walk in the park—if that park were filled with excruciating pain and the constant fear of the unknown. I spent two days in the hospital, enduring a barrage of tests and exams as if the doctors were determined to uncover some hidden super-power that had allowed me to bring this tiny human into the world.

The nurses kept suggesting that I let Drew sleep in the nursery with the other babies so that I could get some much-needed rest. But my little guy was like a koala, content only when he was snuggled up against me. And who was I to deny him? We were already a team, after all.

When he finally drifted off to sleep, I'd tried to nap myself, but my mind was always racing, marveling at the incredible journey that had brought us to this moment. It was as if the universe had looked down at me, chuckled, and said, "Buckle up, buttercup. You're in for the ride of your life."

Looking back, I realize Drew came into my life when I needed him most. After years of pouring my heart and soul into starting my organization in Ghana, I often found myself on the brink of throwing in the towel, ready to book a one-way ticket back to the States. But then, as if by some cosmic intervention, I discovered I was pregnant.

Drew became my anchor, my reason to keep pushing forward even when the waters got choppy. He kept me grounded then, and he keeps me grounded now, a constant reminder of what truly matters in this crazy, beautiful life.

As for my second born, my darling daughter. Well, let's just say she keeps me on my toes in an entirely different way. But more on that later.

Our American sojourn lasted for another whopping three months, thanks in no small part to my mother's deep-seated fear of traveling with a newborn. That, and her unwavering belief in the power of baby chub. In the US, people have this fascination with chunky babies, as if a few extra rolls are the key to lifelong happiness and success.

At birth, Drew weighed in at a respectable seven pounds, seven ounces—not exactly a lightweight, if you ask me. But my mother? She was determined to fatten him up like a prized turkey before Thanksgiving. In her mind, we couldn't possibly return to Ghana without a baby who was the epitome of health and vitality, a veritable poster child for the benefits of American cuisine.

So, for three long months, we lingered in the land of the free and the home of the brave, watching as Drew grew rounder and more adorable with each passing day. When we finally did make our triumphant return to Ghana, we were met with a cultural conundrum.

The act of naming a child in Ghana is not just a personal choice; it's a communal one, a way of welcoming a new life into the fold of family and tradition. And so, when Andy's family seemed hesitant to take on the responsibility of the naming ceremony, it struck a chord of discord, a note of unease in an otherwise joyous time.

I could see the frustration in my mother's eyes, the sense of disappointment that this moment, so crucial to our cultural identity, was not being embraced with the enthusiasm it deserved. It was a reminder that even in the midst of our most cherished traditions, there can be bumps in the road and obstacles to overcome.

We fiercely desired to give Drew a name that would anchor him to his roots, that would connect him to the generations that had come before. And so, with the blessings of our ancestors and the strength of our family, we gave him a name that would forever tie him to the tapestry of our history, a name that would remind him of the love and resilience that had brought him into this world.

On his father's side, tradition dictates that a child must be named within a week of birth. The Ashanti people, bless their patient hearts, grant a little more leeway—two weeks, give or take. But here we were, three months later, still referring to my son as "the baby," as if he were some sort of tiny, unnamed celebrity.

The pressure was on to hold a naming ceremony, to introduce our bundle of joy to the world and bestow upon him a moniker that would shape his destiny. We found ourselves caught in a delicate dance of cultural expectations and familial politics, navigating the complex waters of tradition and modern-day realities. But through it all, one thing remained constant: our love and adoration for our son, who had already captured our hearts and changed our lives in ways we never could have imagined.

We found ourselves navigating the age-old dance of cultural traditions and modern-day realities. In our world, it's the father who holds the sacred duty of naming the child, a responsibility as old as time itself. But here's the thing: we'd already chosen our son's name and etched it onto his birth certificate before we even left the hospital. Drew's identity was set in stone, or so we thought. But in the eyes of our families and the wider community, the baby remained a mystery, a tiny enigma waiting to be unveiled. For them, the naming ceremony was more than just a formality; it was a rite of passage, a moment of great significance that would shape our son's place in the world.

As the days turned into weeks, the pressure mounted. My mother and I found ourselves in the uncomfortable position of pushing for this ceremony, a task that should have fallen squarely on the shoulders of Andy's family. In the Ga tradition, the paternal side takes the lead, a stark contrast to the Ashanti ways, where the maternal lineage holds sway.

It was a delicate dance, navigating the expectations and responsibilities of two distinct cultures. Were they not ready, financially or emotionally? Was there some hidden obstacle that we couldn't see? The questions swirled in my mind as we waited, hoping they would step up and embrace their role in this joyous occasion.

Finally, a date was set, the celebration to be held in the home of the head of my family who is a chief and conveniently lives in Accra. We moved forward with the naming in my family's home. And yet, even then, the burden seemed to fall on us, the women, to make it happen. My mother, Andy's mother, and I spearheaded the coordination. It felt like an uphill battle, a struggle to assert our place in a world that often favors the patriarchal.

But through it all, one thing remained clear: we would move mountains to give Drew the life he deserved, even if it meant challenging the traditions that had shaped our upbringing. In the end, it's the love and strength of a family that truly matters.

It wasn't until about six weeks after our return to Ghana that the long-awaited naming ceremony finally took place. The setting was the home of my mother's second cousin, the Chief, a man of great importance and influence in the Ashanti community. My father, who was not there, had given his authority or rights that he would have as a father, for myself and my sister to our family head, my second mother's cousin, the Chief. He had graciously offered his abode in Accra for the occasion, which spoke volumes about his support for our growing family. He was appointed Chief because he was so good at bringing people together and resolving conflict. This was his stock in trade.

This man, a pillar of strength and wisdom, had stepped into the role of father figure for my sister and me. He carried this responsibility with grace and dignity, a mantle passed down from my dad through the complex tapestry of our family ties.

The chief himself was a force to be reckoned with, a businessman who had spent years abroad honing his skills and expanding his horizons. When he finally returned to Ghana, it was to take up the mantle of chieftaincy, a role he seemed destined to fulfill.

His title, "NkabomHene," spoke to his greatest strength: the ability to bring people together, bridge divides, and heal wounds. In our language, he was known as the "Unifier," a testament to his uncanny knack for fostering harmony and understanding in even the most challenging circumstances.

As he stood there, representing my father and all the generations that had come before us, I couldn't help but feel a sense of awe and gratitude. Here's was a man who had taken on the weight of our family's legacy and stepped up to guide us through the complex dance of tradition and modernity. It was a day steeped in tradition, a moment when our son would be presented to the world—or at least to the intimate gathering of our two families.

And so, with the blessings of our chief and the love of our families, we officially welcomed Drew into the world, secure in the knowledge that he would always have a place to call home, a community to embrace him, and a legacy of unity and strength to guide him through all the years to come.

In our world, naming a child is an act steeped

in meaning and tradition, a far cry from the casual approach often seen in America. A couple might simply decide on a name they like, bestowing it upon their little one with a sense of breezy nonchalance. But for us, the process is so much more profound, a way of connecting our children to the generations that came before them.

Take my own story, for example. I was named after my father's grandmother- Nyarko, a woman who had been the guiding light in his life, a beacon of love and strength through all his trials and tribulations. For him, naming his firstborn daughter after her was a way of honoring her memory, of keeping her spirit alive in the next generation.

And now, that same name, Nyarko, and legacy has been passed down to my son. It's a gift from my father, a piece of his heart that will live on through my little boy. I can only hope that the qualities that made my great-grandmother so special—her kindness, her resilience, her unwavering love—will find their way into my son's soul, guiding him through all the joys and challenges that lie ahead.

I'M AN ASHANTI WOMAN born and raised in Kumasi, the vibrant capital of the Ashanti region in southern Ghana. The Ashanti people are known for their strong work ethic and industrious nature, which have shaped who I am today. I plan to instill these values in my own children as I navigate the journey of parenthood.

When I was just five years old, my father made the difficult decision to leave Ghana and work in Holland. He was driven by the desire to provide a better life for our family, and although it wasn't easy for him to leave us behind, we understood the sacrifice he was making.

Five years later, a remarkable twist of fate changed our lives forever. My mother won the US immigration visa lottery, an opportunity that seemed almost too good to be true. With renewed hope, my father returned from Holland, and together, we embarked on a new chapter in the United States.

We were fortunate to have a comfortable life in Ghana. As the children of two bankers, we were part of the upper-middle class. But more than the material comforts, the strength of our family bond truly defined us.

Growing up Ashanti, I learned invaluable lessons about hard work, perseverance, and resilience. I want to pass on these qualities to my children, the same way my parents and my community instilled them in me.

As I reflect on my own journey, I'm filled with gratitude for the experiences that have shaped me. I know that the path I've chosen as a parent won't always be easy, but I'm confident that with the love and support of my family, and the unwavering spirit I've inherited from my Ashanti heritage, I'll be able to guide my children through whatever challenges life may bring.

During my childhood in Kumasi, the capital of the Ashanti region, I was fortunate to attend private schools. Looking back, I realize that I was somewhat sheltered from the realities of traditional African life. Our family had a driver who would take us to and from school, a luxury that reflected our upper-middle-class status.

Andy came from a different background. While his father worked for the Ministry of Health, his mother didn't have much formal education. There's a noticeable mismatch in our families' social standing. We were distinctly middle class and, although his father's tenure with the Ministry of Health brought in a sizable income, his many siblings were a hefty strain on the family's finances.

I've often heard people make generalizations about the Ga people, the ethnic group he belongs to. They have a reputation for being lazy, and I've lost count of the number of times people have tried to "warn" me about them, saying things like, "Let me give you advice about those Ga people." But I know these stereotypes, while not entirely baseless, are rooted in lived experiences and don't define individuals.

Andy and I complemented each other in many ways, and he has been my best friend for a long time. In fact, he's the reason I stayed in Ghana, even though I found it challenging to adapt at times. Making friends as an adult in a new place is never easy, and for about a year, we relied heavily on each other for companionship. We lived in a secluded, up-and-coming area in the Greater Accra region, which meant we had to drive everywhere to socialize. The isolation from the hustle and bustle of the city was welcomed by both of us, but it wasn't practical for our relationship. We probably held onto each other longer than we should have. We were together for nearly eight years, but eventually realized that we couldn't keep going back and forth.

I fell in love with him through work when I moved back to Ghana years ago. He is nine years younger than me, and I was initially hesitant about the relationship, especially since I was his boss at the time.

As a person with a disability, I faced my own set of challenges when it came to starting a family. I kept both of my pregnancies secret from most of my extended family, as I didn't want to face the stigma and questions about my ability to deliver and raise a child. However, I was determined to learn how to change a diaper with one hand and to breastfeed my babies.

Every experience, every relationship, and every challenge has played a role in shaping the woman I am today. But I should go back in time to tell you about that fateful day when I was 18. Little did I know that my life was about to take a drastic turn, one that would test my resilience and determination like never before. The events that unfolded on that day would forever alter the course of my journey, leaving me to navigate a new reality and discover depths of strength I never knew I possessed.

CHAPTER 2

# The Accident

IT WAS A QUAKER BOARDING SCHOOL in Westchester,
Pennsylvania—a place that seemed as serene and timeless
as a Norman Rockwell painting, that became the setting
from where I would experience my most life-changing
event. Westtown School, with its whispering trees and
ancient stone buildings, felt like a world away from the
all-girls Catholic school in Brooklyn and in Ghana where
a good part of my childhood had played out like a strict,
silent film. Before my transfer to Westtown, my sister
had been approached by a nonprofit organization called
the Teak Fellowship. They scouted students from low-income areas, offering them a golden ticket to private high
schools and, with any luck, prestigious colleges. When
my father saw this opportunity for my sister, he nudged
me toward the same path.

My education at Westtown was a unique blend of
hard work and humility. Unlike some of the prestigious
boarding schools my friends attended, where wealth
was on full display, my school took a different approach.

Nestled on a sprawling campus, Westtown had a small farm where we grew our own food, and every student was expected to contribute.

Westtown School

We called them "jobs" or "work," and each semester, we were assigned different tasks. Some of us would plant the crops, while others would take on the responsibility of harvesting. It was a far cry from the experience my sister had at St. Paul's School in Massachusetts, where the cleaning staff would tidy up after the students. At Westtown, we had to make our own beds and keep the common spaces clean.

With the hindsight of maturity, I realize now that this experience, while perhaps not as glamorous as some other prep schools, taught me valuable lessons. It humbled me and instilled a strong work ethic that I carry with me to this day.

Westtown's Quaker values were evident in the simplicity of the school environment. There weren't many ornaments or ostentatious displays of wealth. It reminded me of the stories you hear about Bill Gates, one of the richest people in the world, still getting a $5 or $10 haircut. The school had its fair share of wealthy students, some from families with old money, but you wouldn't know it from walking around the campus.

One of my classmates was the grandson of the Tylenol fortune, and my own roommate came from a wealthy background. But at Westtown, everyone was treated the same. It was a refreshing change from my sister's school, where the abundance of money was palpable.

In my native language, we have a saying, "Dwen Wo Ho," which roughly translates to "minding our own business." That's the vibe I got from Westtown. They didn't feel the need to flaunt their wealth or make a big deal out of who was who. Everyone was there to mind their business, to learn, to grow, and to contribute to the community.

As a minority student on scholarship, I knew I had to work hard to maintain my place at the school. There were countless other deserving black and brown kids waiting for an opportunity like mine, so I threw myself into every aspect of campus life. I knew that I couldn't take my education for granted, and I was determined to make the most of it.

The school's emphasis on hard work and equality shaped me into the person I am today. It taught me that true wealth lies not in material possessions or flashy displays, but in the strength of character and the willingness to put in the effort to achieve one's goals. This ethos resonated for me early in my life and interestingly, has become the core of who I am. Little did I know when I started there how much I was going to need to draw on those principles before I was barely launched into young adulthood.

Life at Westtown was messy and unpredictable, but it was mine, and for the first time, I felt like the main character of my own story. Back in Brooklyn, I had been a sophomore at the local Catholic school, my days filled with uniforms and unyielding discipline, when I applied to Teak. The fellowship, with its benevolent hands, guided me through the application maze and ensured I could attend Westtown with the necessary financial aid. To maximize this aid, I repeated my sophomore year. It was a strategic move, they said, giving me time to adjust to the academic rigors of my new world and excel. I needed that year to blend in, to fit into a puzzle where the pieces were a little more jagged than I was used to.

Life up to this point had been all about Catholic

schools. Now, for the first time, I was stepping into a coeducational setting, far from home. It was liberating and terrifying in equal measure. Freedoms I had never imagined were now within my grasp. Had I stayed in Brooklyn, I would have continued to be the prim and proper daughter, dutifully meeting my parents' expectations.

But at Westown, things were different. There were boys, lots of them. For the first time, I was no longer cloistered in a sea of plaid skirts and nuns. As a 15- or 16-year-old girl, suddenly thrust into this new co-ed environment, I found the attention intoxicating. It was as if I had been handed the script for a romantic comedy, and I was determined to play the lead.

My new friends introduced me to a world beyond the confining walls of my previous life. One afternoon, beneath the venerable oaks, I smoked weed for the first time, giggling with friends from the track and cross-country teams. I maintained my grades of course—dropping my GPA would have been tantamount to mutiny—but outside the classroom, I allowed myself to explore the uncharted territories of teenage rebellion. The parents of my new friends, however, operated under a different set of rules. At their houses they were allowed to drink and smoke as long as it was under their roof. I never really got to experience this level of freedom or parental benign neglect, as to do so would have required a permission slip from my parents which I knew there was no point in asking for. The answer would have been a swift 'NO'.

And then, there was the matter of boys. I had my first boyfriend, a nerdy but cute guy from the baseball team, Dell, who expressed interest within weeks of my arrival. This new chapter of my life was a whirlwind of emotions and experiences, each one shaping me in ways I had never anticipated.

Neither Dell nor I had access to a car so our brief 'relationship' was a very local one, relegated mostly to meet-ups post-study hall in the evenings or on campus on the weekends.

I think I was the first girl who gave Dell any attention at all, so it didn't escalate to anything sexual. And then, another guy who also ran track and played baseball showed interest in me. And at 16 years old, I lost my virginity to him. My mother especially made me and my sister promise that we would wait till we were at least 18 before we had sex, but then it just happened.

Westtown School was sprawling, with acres of land that seemed to stretch on forever. At the time, they were only using a portion of it for classrooms and dorms. I lived in the girls' dorm, separated from the boys by a respectable distance. As a transfer student, I had a roommate named Claren. She came from a family with a notable lineage—the founders of the Audubon Society. Despite her wealthy background, she was incredibly modest. You would never know she was wealthy just by looking at her.

We came from completely different worlds. I shared a small apartment with my mom, dad, and sister in Brooklyn. Claren, on the other hand, invited me to her family's house in Connecticut for our first winter break. It was there that I discovered the extent of her family's legacy. Their home was adorned with bird-themed art and memorabilia, a nod to their Audubon heritage.

During that winter break, I experienced a world I had only seen in movies. We went skiing, and although I had seen snow in New York, this was my first time on a ski slope. It was as if my eyes were being opened to a new, dazzling world. Claren's family also took me horseback riding for the first time. These were activities I had never imagined doing, coming from my modest background.

This boarding school experience exposed me to people and opportunities I would never have encountered otherwise. It was a privilege to be part of such a diverse environment at a young age, broadening my horizons in ways I had never thought possible.

One school vacation, I came home and announced to my parents that I didn't want to eat meat anymore—I wanted to be a vegetarian. This was met with significant resistance, to put it mildly. My parents saw it as yet another sign that I was being influenced by "white people" and their strange ideas. To them, my new dietary preference was just another form of rebellion against the way they had raised me.

## In the Blink of an Eye

THE DAY OF THE ACCIDENT was a special day, a celebration of my friend Kate's birthday. Kate was a fellow member of the track and cross-country teams, and we had all decided to mark the occasion with a dinner outing. The memories of that day are hazy now, but I do remember the excitement we felt as we made our plans.

We had asked one of our favorite teachers, Chisa, to join us. Chisa was an African American woman, fresh out of college at just 21 or 22 years old, and she had already made a profound impact on us as our Theater Arts teacher. She also taught an advanced English class and offered electives that we eagerly signed up for.

There was something magnetic about Chisa. Perhaps it was the fact that she was so close to us in age, or maybe it was her cool, approachable demeanor. Whatever the reason, we all gravitated towards her, always seeking out her company and guidance. As a young black girl myself, I saw Chisa as a role model, someone to look up to and emulate.

When we asked Chisa if she would be willing to drive us to the restaurant for Kate's birthday dinner, she readily agreed. We piled into the van, chattering excitedly about the evening ahead. The details of what happened next are a bit blurry in my mind. I can't quite remember if we were on our way to the restaurant or heading back to campus when the accident occurred.

From what I've pieced together through conversations with the others who were with me that night, it seems that something unexpected happened on the road. Some say it was raining heavily, while others recall an animal, possibly a deer, darting across our path. Whatever the cause, Chisa suddenly swerved, losing control of the van.

In a heartbeat, my life changed forever. The van veered off the road, and I found myself in a terrifying situation. Sitting near the window–no seat belts back then, I was ejected from the vehicle as it careened out of control. My upper body was thrown from the window, while my legs, from the waist down, remained trapped inside the van.

The horror of what followed is still difficult to comprehend, all these years later. The van collapsed on top of me, crushing the right side of my head and fracturing my skull.

In the aftermath of the accident, I learned that I was the only one who had suffered such severe injuries. My friends, including the one who had been sitting right next to me, were all released from the hospital after an overnight stay. They returned to campus the very next day, while I was lying in a coma, my family not even sure if I was going to survive.

The extent of my injuries was severe, and the medical team had to make a crucial decision. In order to allow room for my brain to swell and ensure that enough oxygen could reach it, they removed a piece of my skull. It was a drastic measure, but one that ultimately helped to stabilize my condition.

Once I was deemed stable enough, I was transferred to the Children's Hospital of Philadelphia. It seemed that the accident had occurred while we were either near Philly or on our way back to Westchester, Pennsylvania. The proximity to Philadelphia had played a role in the decision to take us to a hospital in that area.

During my stay at the Children's Hospital, I underwent a series of treatments and procedures. Blood transfusions were a critical part of my care, as the doctors worked to replenish what I had lost in the accident. It was during this time that a revelation came to light.

According to my sister, who learned of this after the fact, the hospital had conducted blood work as part of my treatment. The results showed traces of marijuana in my system, a discovery that sent shockwaves through my family. Suddenly, the focus shifted from my physical recovery to the choices I had been making at school.

My parents were understandably concerned, not

only about the severity of my injuries but also about the implications of my drug use. It was as if they believed that my experimentation with pot had somehow contributed to the accident, a notion that I knew to be untrue.

I never told my mother that I kept a diary, which to be fair, is the point of diaries. Writing had always been my way of making sense of the world—a private sanctuary where I could process the whirlwind of changes in my life. Little did I know that this diary would eventually betray me. After the accident, while I was in a coma, my family had to clean out my dorm room. That's when they discovered the diary. I'm told that it was my sister who went to my dorm and cleared out my things. I imagine my parents sifting through them later on and stumbling upon the book that held all my secrets. To them, it must have been like finding a time bomb.

For me, writing was a refuge. I loved to write, always have. It was my way of understanding the new experiences and changes happening around me. But that diary, filled with my deepest thoughts and teenage indiscretions, became a weapon in my parents' hands. My dad, especially, felt betrayed. He had invested so much in my sister and me, and my diary entries made him feel I had thrown it all away. When I finally woke up from the six-week coma, everyone was relieved that I survived. But the elephant in the room, my diary, was never addressed directly. It was an unspoken tension, a silent storm brewing in our household.

For a long time, I felt like my parents believed I deserved the accident and that it was some cosmic punishment for my teenage rebellion. Even though I maintained a B+ average, enough to keep my scholarship, it wasn't the straight-A performance they had come to expect. Their disappointment lingered, a shadow over my achievements.

Despite everything, I have come to realize that life's journey is never a straight path. It's filled with twists, turns, and unexpected detours. And sometimes, those detours, painful as they may be, are the ones that lead us to the most profound truths.

## The Long Road

For nearly two years, the Children's Hospital became my home. I spent six weeks in a coma, a period of time that remains a blank slate in my memory. I have no recollection of anything that happened while I was unconscious, lost in a world of darkness and silence.

As I began to emerge from the coma, I remember feeling a sense of confusion and disorientation. The drowsiness that accompanied my gradual awakening made it difficult to distinguish between reality and the fragments of dreams that seemed to linger in my mind.

I recall my family discussing the possibility of moving from our apartment in Brooklyn, a topic that had been on the table for some time. In my hazy state, I couldn't help but wonder if we had already made that move. Everything felt different, unfamiliar.

It was during the first weekend after I regained consciousness that my father had taken a brief respite from his constant vigil at my bedside. My mother was the only one with me when I finally spoke my first words: "Where's Dad?"

From that moment on, the questions tumbled out of me, a torrent of confusion and uncertainty. I asked about the move, trying to make sense of my surroundings. The words felt heavy on my tongue as if my brain was struggling to connect the dots between my thoughts and my ability to express them.

As I lay there, grappling with the reality of my situation, I couldn't help but feel a sense of frustration and helplessness. The road ahead seemed long and daunting, but I knew that I had no choice but to face it head-on, one day at a time.

Once I had regained consciousness and started trying to talk again, I would often not be able to find the words to speak. My mother used to tell me that when I was a child, I was quite literally, tongue-tied. And, the only way she discovered that I was tongue-tied was when I had crawled under my crib and she couldn't find me for hours. I wasn't crying or making a sound. When they finally found me, they thought surely something was wrong with me and they rushed me to the hospital, which is where they discovered that there was a band of tissue under my tongue that was unusually thick and clamping my tongue to the bottom of my mouth, rendering me unable to make sound. Looking back, it seems like there are repeating patterns in my life.

It took me six weeks to two months to be able to start speaking somewhat normally again after I came out of the coma. I was able to form and speak simple sentences but deeper thought required cognitive remediation and more speech therapy. During that time, my entire world revolved around the almighty thumb. It was like I had been transported back to ancient Rome, where the fate of gladiators was decided by the simple up or down motion of a digit. Except in my case, it wasn't about life or death, but rather about the basic necessities of human existence.

My therapists became masters of the thumb-based language, rapid-firing questions like they were auditioning for a role in a high-stakes charades tournament. "Give me a thumbs up if you need to use the bathroom. Number 1? Number 2? Thumbs down if you're all good. And if it's somewhere in between, just leave that thumb hovering in no man's land."

I felt like I was playing the world's most intense game of "Hot or Cold," except instead of searching for a hidden object, I was trying to communicate my bodily functions. But then, like a knight in shining armor, my cognitive therapist swooped in with pen and paper. Suddenly, I was back in the game, scribbling away like a madman. It was a good thing the accident had left my right hand unscathed, or else I would have been reduced to writing with my toes.

For two months, I survived on this bizarre combination of nonverbal thumbs-up, thumbs-down communication, and frantic note-writing. It was like living in a silent movie, minus the charming black-and-white filter and the jaunty piano soundtrack.

And then, one day, a miracle happened. Words began to tumble out of my mouth like clumsy acrobats, somersaulting into sentences before I even realized what was happening.

I have what the medical experts call an "acquired traumatic brain injury," or TBI for short. Remember how I mentioned they removed part of my skull so that my brain could safely swell? Believe it or not, they actually stored a piece of my skull in the fridge for safekeeping. I guess they wanted to make sure it stayed fresh, like a container of leftover guacamole.

After about a year or so, they decided it was time to put the puzzle pieces of my skull back together. They took that chilled skull fragment out of cold storage, probably gave it a quick once-over, and then proceeded to cement it back in place. It was like a game of surgical Tetris, trying to get everything to fit just right.

During this surgery, they not only put the skull piece back where it belonged but also did a bit of reconstructive surgery and skin grafting for good measure. Skin grafting is basically like a tiny transplant. They took some skin from another part of my body and moved it to the right side of my head, where I had lost a bit of my hair due to the accident. It was like a miniature version of a hair restoration procedure, except instead of giving me a luscious mane, they were just trying to make sure I didn't have any bald patches.

All of this happened while I was trying to finish high school and start college part-time. Talk about multitasking. I was juggling inpatient stays at the children's hospital for about a year, then outpatient therapies for another year. I had speech therapy, occupational therapy, physical therapy—it was like a full-time job, except instead of a paycheck, I was just trying to get my brain and body back in working order.

The whole point of this medical adventure was to get me to a place where I could start to focus on living at least a relatively normal life again. I was facing the prospect of new horizons—Hunter College in Manhattan in the fall—even if it was just part-time and I had to live at home—it was the first step towards the independent adult life I was so deeply craving.

# CHAPTER 3

# The Long Road Through Rehab

As I navigated the unfamiliar waters of my recovery, Philadelphia became my temporary harbor. From there, I embarked on a journey that would take me back and forth between New York and Philadelphia every couple of weeks, each trip a testament to my determination to heal.

The rhythm of my life became dictated by therapy sessions—speech, cognitive remediation, occupational therapy. These became the building blocks of my new reality, each one a step towards reclaiming the independence I had lost. My speech therapist, in particular, became more than just a medical professional. She morphed into a guide, helping me to navigate not just words, but the complex path back to a semblance of normalcy.

As the possibility of returning to school full-time loomed on the horizon, our sessions took on new urgency. We worked tirelessly on cognitive exercises, each one designed to prepare me for the challenges that lay ahead. Meanwhile, my occupational therapist patiently helped me relearn the basics of daily life—dressing, bathing, the simple acts that most take for granted but had become monumental one-handed tasks for me.

In the sterile halls of hospitals and therapy rooms, I found an unexpected warmth. My therapists became more than healthcare providers; they became my friends, filling the void left by the life I had lost. Kripa, my PT in Philadelphia, with her gentle Indian accent and unwavering encouragement, became a beacon of hope. Tami, my occupational therapist, with her patient guidance, became a cornerstone of my recovery.

Years later, as I stood on the precipice of motherhood, I felt an overwhelming urge to reconnect with these people who had been so instrumental in my healing. I wanted them to see how far I had come, to show them that their efforts had not been in vain. Walking through the halls of the Children's Hospital of Philadelphia, now as an expectant mother rather than a broken teenager, I felt a profound sense of gratitude and accomplishment.

As I juggled outpatient therapy with part-time classes at Hunter College, my mother, Mary, became my constant companion, my "aide" as we jokingly called her. She had quit her job to be by my side, helping me navigate the subway, guiding me through campus life, and accompanying me not only to therapy sessions but to my classes. In her sacrifice, I found strength, in her unwavering support, I found the courage to keep pushing forward.

This journey of recovery was not just about healing my body and mind. It was about rediscovering myself, rebuilding relationships, and finding a new purpose in life. Each therapy session, each class, and each small victory was a sign that I could do it, I had to keep putting one foot in front of the other. As I look back on those challenging days, I realize that they were not just about recovery, but about rebirth—the emergence of a new self, stronger and more determined than ever before.

IN THE WAKE OF MY ACCIDENT, a strange alchemy occurred—tragedy forged a bond between my mother and me that had been missing for years. Before that fateful day, we had been living parallel lives.A former banker in Ghana, my parents made the decision for her to work in New Jersey as home health aide because this would make more money and bring us closer to the goal of returning to Ghana., Her presence in our home was marked by sporadic visits, while my father shouldered the day-to-day responsibilities of raising my sister and me.

As a teenager, I had grown accustomed to this arrangement, never fully realizing the void it had created in our relationship. But life has a way of upending our carefully constructed realities, and my accident became the catalyst for a profound transformation.

Suddenly, my mother was there—not just physically, but in every sense of the word. She became my constant companion, my confidante, my lifeline. Every struggle, every small win, every moment of frustration or joy— she was there to witness it all. It was as if the universe had decided to hit the reset button on our relationship, giving us a chance to build something new from the ashes of what had been lost.

Yet, this newfound closeness was not without its complexities. At times, I felt myself leaning on her too heavily, using her as a crutch to bear the weight of my frustrations and fears. The normal concerns of a young woman—dating, social life, independence—were over-shadowed by the more pressing need for recovery. And my mother, since she was ever present, became the repository for all my unspoken desires and disappoint-ments. Not to mention, my sometimes less-than-gracious feelings of resentment that I, a young adult woman on the cusp of independence, still needed to rely on my mother to go anywhere or do anything.

Meanwhile, my father, Isaac, found himself thrust into the role of provider with a renewed sense of urgency. As insurance companies threatened to withdraw their support, sending ominous notices about the cost of my care, he redoubled his efforts at work. His focus became singular: to ensure that we would have the resources to continue my treatment, even if the official support was cut off.

It was a stark contrast to their lives in Ghana, where both my parents had been respected bankers, providing us with a comfortable middle-class lifestyle. In the US, they had to reinvent themselves. My mother's journey took her from being a cashier at Bronx Community College to a position at Citibank, and finally to working as a home health aide. The latter job often took her away from us for months at a time, living with her elderly patients in New Jersey.

My father, meanwhile, found work as a supervisor at the Jacob Javits Convention Center in New York. It was steady work, more "respectable" perhaps than my mother's, but it came with its own pressures and demands.

Through it all, my mother bore the emotional burden for both my sister and me. She became our rock, our confidante, our everything. It was a role thrust upon her by circumstance and cultural expectations, but one she embraced with a strength I had never fully appreciated before.

As I look back on that time, we forged a new kind of family dynamic—one built on shared struggle, unwavering support, and a depth of understanding that we had never known before. It wasn't always easy, and the road ahead was still long and uncertain, but we were facing it together. And in that togetherness, I found a strength I never knew I possessed.

THE RHYTHM OF MY RECOVERY was marked by the steady beat of therapy sessions. Three times a week, I would make my way to physical therapy, a journey that became as familiar as the lines on my palm. The hospital tried to schedule everything on the same day, a small mercy that saved me from the exhaustion of constant back-and-forth trips.

However it was the journey to Hunter College that truly tested my newfound limitations. As I said, my mother accompanied me to every class, a silent sentinel waiting outside as I navigated the unfamiliar world of higher education. The campus, with its modern architecture of glass and steel, became an unexpected challenge.

My first sociology class was mercifully on the ground floor, but as I added more courses, I found myself faced with a daunting obstacle—the glass bridge walkway connecting different buildings. It was here that the true extent of my injuries became apparent. The accident left me with a fear of heights and a disorienting sense of spatial awareness that I had never experienced before.

Stepping onto that bridge was like stepping into a waking nightmare. My body would betray me, hands and legs shaking as if I were standing on the edge of a precipice rather than a secure walkway. In those moments, Mom's presence was my lifeline. She would walk beside me, a steady hand to guide me across, her quiet strength a counterpoint to my trembling uncertainty.

As time passed and I grew more confident, I found my own ways to cope. Instead of braving the bridge, I would leave the building and cross at street level. Even years later, my gait marked by a persistent limp, I would make this journey. In the bustling streets of New York, where everyone seemed to be racing against an invisible clock, I moved at my own pace. Slowly, steadily, I would make my way across the impatient city swirling around me like a river around a stone.

My mother remained my backup, my security in this new world I was learning to navigate. In her watchful gaze, I reflected both the person I had been and the person I was becoming—a survivor learning to thrive in a world that had suddenly become much more complex. In my quieter moments of reflection, I understand the logic of gratitude. My mind can comprehend the necessity of the assistance I received, the unwavering support that carried me through the darkest days of my recovery. But the heart, oh, the heart of a 20-year-old yearning for independence, that's a different story altogether. I had

tasted freedom before the accident and knew the exhila-
ration of living on my own terms. To have that snatched
away, to find myself dependent once more, was a bitter pill to swallow. The frustration of those days lingers
even now, at 39, a ghostly echo of my younger self's
rebellion.

Just this morning, as my children and I prepared
for a trip to the lake, I felt that old tension resurface.
By 8:30, we were ready, excitement bubbling in the air.
But my mother, insisting on joining us, was nowhere to
be seen. As 10:30 rolled around and we sat waiting, I
could feel the familiar irritation rising within me. It's
a delicate dance, this balance between appreciation
and frustration. I know I'm capable, yet her overprotec-
tiveness, born of love and past trauma, often feels like
shackles holding me back.

As I try to entertain my restless 3-year-old and
5-year-old, I can't help but ponder the irony of our situation. My mother, now in her early 60s, resists getting a
driver or driving herself, leaving us perpetually waiting,
and adjusting our schedules to accommodate her. Her
complaints of sleepless nights seem to coincide with my
presence as if her body remembers the long vigils of my
recovery. When I ask for her help, her response is often,
"I didn't sleep well last night," or "I'm just catching up
on sleep now." It's hard not to interpret these words as a
subtle reminder of her sacrifices, a gentle nudge toward

guilt. And so, I find myself caught in a cycle of frustration and accommodation. The organized, efficient part of me chafes against the delays and adjustments, while the other part recognizes the deep-seated fears and love that drive her actions.

In these moments, I'm reminded that healing is not a straight line. It's a winding path that affects not just the injured, but those who love them as well. And sometimes, the hardest part of recovery is learning to navigate these new dynamics, to find a balance between gratitude and independence, between the person you were and the person you've become.

When the hustle of daily life subsides, I often find myself grappling with a peculiar kind of guilt. It's a feeling that sneaks up on me, whispering reminders of all that my family has done for me. "I was there for you when you were dying," it seems to say. "I've been there for you when you were having your kids." And with each reminder, I feel the weight of an unspoken debt growing heavier on my shoulders.

But then, in moments of clarity, I push back against this notion. "What you've done," I want to tell them, "Is what any family would do." Isn't it the natural response when a loved one faces a near-death experience? To rally together, to fight for their survival, to ensure they have the best chance at life. It's not exceptional—at least it shouldn't be. It should be what family means.

Yet, the expectation to overcompensate lingers, manifesting in ways both big and small. There's the monthly stipend from my settlement after the accident, a gesture of support based on the assumption that I might never lead a full, independent life. While I'm grateful for this cushion, it sometimes feels like a reminder of what could have been, rather than what is.

Then there are the more personal instances. My sister's student loans, for example. No one explicitly asked me to help, but there was an unspoken expectation that I would clear her debt, allowing her to start her professional life unencumbered. And I did, because that's what family does, isn't it?

But it's the smaller things that often speak the loudest. My mother borrows my sunglasses, and then keeps them without a word, as if my ability to replace them negates the need to return them. Or the time she asked me to book flights for a family wedding ceremony in Nigeria, promising to pay me back—a promise that has since transformed into a belief that repayment isn't necessary.

These moments, these small acts of taking without giving back, add up. They create a tapestry of expectation and obligation that sometimes feels suffocating. It's as if my survival, my recovery, has become a debt that can never truly be repaid.

And yet, even as I struggle with these feelings, I'm

reminded of the depth of love that underlies it all. The same love that drove my family to fight for my survival now manifests in these complicated, sometimes frustrating ways. It's a reminder that healing isn't just about physical recovery—it's about navigating the complex web of relationships that have been forever changed by trauma.

In the end, I find myself seeking a balance. A way to honor the sacrifices my family has made without losing myself in the process. To be grateful for their support while also asserting my independence. It's a delicate dance, one that I'm still learning to master, even all these years later.

In the tapestry of family dynamics, there are threads that bind us together and others that tangle, creating knots of tension and unspoken expectations. My relationship with my mother and sister has become one such complicated weave.

My sister, successful in her own right with a six-figure job at Microsoft, seems to exist in a different realm in my mother's eyes. When it comes to requests for money or even small favors like borrowing sunglasses, my mother's gaze invariably turns to me. Sometimes it feels like my recovery has quietly placed me in the role of family supporter, in ways I didn't quite expect.

My mother's friend was visiting from Ghana not long ago. I had arranged for some supplements to be brought over, and suddenly, my mother saw an opportunity. She began listing additional items she wanted me to purchase as if my resources were limitless. When I suggested she ask my sister Agatha for help, it became a point of contention.

Perhaps it's because Agatha will always be the baby in my mother's eyes. Or maybe it's because I've inadvertently set a precedent. While I've always been glad to support my family, the ways I've done so have, at times, created a complex dynamic I'm still learning to navigate.

But the weight of these expectations has begun to feel oppressive. The reality is, that I'm not financially leagues above the rest of my family. I'm a mother now, with my own children to consider. The luxury of carefree spending and travel is mine to claim but I shouldn't be expected to care for my extended family.

I find myself constantly torn between gratitude for my family's support during my recovery and the need to establish boundaries. When I recently drafted my will, my mother's hurt at what she perceived as denial of what was due to her, felt like a knife twisting in my heart. The subsequent conversation with my sister about removing her from the annual trust payments was equally challenging.

"Why?" my sister kept asking. "Why not just keep me on it?"

I struggled to make her understand that her six-figure

salary negated the need for my continued financial support. But people grow accustomed to certain comforts, and change, even when necessary, is rarely welcomed with open arms.

As I navigate these choppy waters of familial expectations and personal boundaries, I'm reminded of a lesson I learned during my recovery: healing isn't just about physical rehabilitation. It's about recalibrating relationships, reassessing priorities, and sometimes, making difficult decisions for the greater good.

The path forward isn't clear, but I know that I must find a way to honor the sacrifices my family has made for me while also securing a stable future for my own children. It's a delicate balance, one that requires courage, compassion, and above all, honest communication. In the end, I hope we can weave a new pattern in our family tapestry, one that respects each member's needs and celebrates our collective strength.

In the intricate dance of family relationships, there are steps that feel familiar and others that catch you off guard, leaving you struggling to find your balance. My journey with my parents has been one such complicated waltz.

When Andy of eight years, the father of my children, finally asked for my hand in marriage, I expected joy. Instead, my mother's first words were, "You need to get a prenup." The irony wasn't lost on me—I doubt she'd ever uttered those words to my sister. It was as if my recovery had transformed me into a valuable asset that needed protection, rather than a daughter seeking happiness.

This dynamic of unequal expectations played out again when my family started a company in Ghana. My parents pooled their resources, and I contributed significantly. But when my father divorced my mother and remarried, he suddenly wanted out of the family and the business we'd built in Ghana. . He presented me with a bill so outrageous, it was as if he'd poured his entire life into this venture and had nothing left.

We negotiated, my mother, acting as an expected ally, crossed out inflated figures until we reached an agreement. I paid him out, hoping it would bring closure. But family debts, it seems, are never truly settled.

Not long after, I found my father struggling in the US. Without hesitation, I paid his rent for a year. It wasn't a loan or an investment—it was simply what a family does. Yet, in a twist that left me reeling, he later claimed I had never done anything for him.

These moments leave me questioning the nature of family obligation and gratitude. Is it possible that the very act of surviving my accident, of defying the odds and building a life for myself, has somehow indebted me to my family in ways I can never repay? Or is this a form of emotional manipulation, a subtle gaslighting that makes me doubt my own memories and efforts?

I'm reminded of a quote from one of my favorite books, Tuesdays with Morrie, by Mitch Albom. Mitch's old professor, Morrie, shares with him this piece of wisdom: "The most important thing in life is to learn how to give out love, and to let it come in." I've thought about this idea a lot throughout my life. I wish Morrie had said more about how challenging it can be when that love comes wrapped in expectations and unspoken debts.

As I navigate these choppy waters of family dynamics, I find myself seeking a balance. I want to honor the sacrifices my family has made for me, to acknowledge the love and support that carried me through my darkest days. But I also need to establish boundaries, to protect the life I've built and the future I envision for my children.

Perhaps the greatest challenge of my recovery hasn't been physical at all. Maybe it's been learning to reconcile the person I was before the accident with the person I've become—and helping my family make that same leap. It's a journey we're still on, filled with missteps and moments of grace, as we learn to dance to this new, complex rhythm of family life.

# CHAPTER 4

# *Embracing Different*

As I was adjusting to my part-time college life, I was also adjusting to my new self-image. I had become a young woman "with a disability." I was struggling to navigate this new life and there was this gray area I was gradually coming to terms with—the reality of what happened to me, but the emotions surrounding it and what it meant for the rest of my life took more time to process than just learning how to walk and talk again.

It's hard to make sense of going from being recruited for the soccer team one day, being knocked out and waking up several weeks later, bedridden, and being told that if I did survive, the best I could hope for was to be a semi-mobile vegetable. The severity of the accident was so extreme that none of the health care professionals, or even my family, could imagine me getting back to some sort of "normal" ever again.

The doctors told my parents, "She will not survive, number one, and if she does survive, she will be a vegetable." I was not supposed to be able to speak, I was not supposed to walk, I was not supposed to do anything that I have been able to do well over the past 22 years. Take what doctors say to you with a grain of salt.

When they gave my parents that diagnosis, I was in a coma, so I wasn't able to hear but hearing it for the first time after I woke up, I was devastated. But after I got over the initial shock, some steely resolve took root in me, and just said, Oh yeah? We'll see about that. People have asked me a lot, "Where do you get the strength to be able to navigate life the way you are?" I am not a very religious person, but my faith is strong. I don't have anything else to attribute my faith in my recovery but to God.

As consciousness slowly returned to me, I found myself adrift in a sea of confusion. My first words, "Where's Dad?" tumbled out, revealing the disorientation that clouded my mind. In my haze, I had concocted a narrative where we had moved from our Brooklyn apartment into a smaller, one-bedroom place. The reality, of course, was far different—we were in a hospital room, surrounded by the trappings of a health care crisis.

The disconnect between my imagined reality and the truth was jarring. As I gazed around the room, taking in the Get-well cards, the flowers, and the constant stream of visitors, I struggled to make sense of my surroundings. It was as if I was viewing the world through a foggy lens, unable to bring anything into sharp focus.

Strangely, no one explicitly told me I had been in an accident. I pieced it together gradually, realizing that something significant had occurred, but the details remained frustratingly out of reach. My memory was a patchwork, with clear recollections of events just before the crash, then nothing until I woke up in the hospital.

Friends from school became regular visitors, their presence a tenuous link to the life I had known before. My high school boyfriend, who had been in the van during the crash but escaped with just a scratch on his knee, came to see me. In a moment of privacy, he asked if I would be able to make it to the prom. The question hung in the air, a painful reminder of the gulf between my current reality and the future I had once envisioned.

Despite my inability to walk, I found myself clinging to the idea of attending these senior-year milestones. I asked my mother to bring my prom dress as if putting it on could transport me back to the life I had lost. In my mind, I was still preparing for all the senior parties and get-togethers, unable or unwilling to fully grasp the severity of my situation.

This cognitive dissonance—the gap between my expectations and my new reality—was perhaps the cruelest aspect of my recovery. It was a constant reminder of all that had been lost, all that had changed in the blink of an eye. As I navigated this confusing new world,

I began to realize that my journey of recovery would be as much about healing my mind and spirit as it was about rehabilitating my body. It was a process of coming to terms with my new reality, of redefining my expectations, and of finding new ways to engage with the world around me.

As my physical therapy evolved and I took my first steps, the gravity of the moment was palpable. My father stood silently nearby, the only family member present for this milestone. I gripped the parallel bars, my lifelines in this new world of rehabilitation, as Kripa gently guided my left leg forward. "Now move right," she encouraged. We repeated this dance, left then right, over and over, until suddenly, I swung my left foot forward on my own.

It was a breakthrough, a moment that should have been celebrated with unbridled joy. Kripa's excitement was evident in her voice as she cheered me on. But my father's response was tellingly different. "Remember, you used to run in high school," he said, his voice steady. "So, keep going and let's get back to running."

His words, well-intentioned as they were, encapsulated our family's approach to adversity. We didn't pause to acknowledge the magnitude of what had happened or to grieve the life I had lost. There was no moment of reflection on our new normal or contemplation of what my future might hold. Instead, we treated my recovery like a checklist, a series of tasks to be completed in order to "get better."

This approach wasn't born of indifference or lack of love. It was simply our way, ingrained in our cultural DNA. Things happen, but we don't talk about them, we don't delve into the whys, hows, and wherefores. We just keep moving forward.

Looking back, I can't help but wonder how different things might have been if we had allowed ourselves to pause, to truly process the seismic shift in our lives. If I were in my parents' shoes now, watching one of my own children take their first steps after months of immobility, I know I would react differently. I would celebrate each small victory, and shower them with praise and encouragement.

But that wasn't our family's way. We didn't sit by our bedsides, engaging in heart-to-heart conversations about feelings and fears. My father and I, despite being the more emotional members of our family, still adhered to this unspoken rule of stoic forward motion.

The accident, life-altering as it was, was treated almost clinically. It happened, it was unfortunate, and now we had to focus on the next steps. Physical therapy, learning to walk, learning to talk—these became our new goals, our new normal. There was no time allocated for discussing the emotional toll, no space created for processing the trauma we had all endured.

In sharing this, I'm not seeking to assign blame

or express regret. It's simply a reflection on the complex dynamics that shape our responses to life's most challenging moments. Our family's approach gave me strength in many ways, pushing me to focus on progress rather than dwelling on what was lost. But it also left certain wounds unaddressed, creating an emotional legacy that I'm still grappling with today.

As I continue on this journey of recovery and self-discovery, I've come to realize that healing isn't just about physical rehabilitation. It's also about acknowledging the pain, the fear, and the grief that come with such a profound life change. It's a lesson I carry with me, influencing how I approach challenges and how I hope to support my own children through their trials.

My PT, Kripa, was more than just a medical professional in my journey of recovery. At 22, she was only a few years older than me, and this closeness in age fostered a bond that transcended the typical patient-therapist relationship.

Fresh out of college and completing her internship in the States, Kripa brought a youthful energy to our sessions that both challenged and comforted me. She became my confidante, helping me navigate not just the physical hurdles of rehabilitation but the mental and emotional obstacles as well.

As the daughter of immigrant parents, Kripa had her own struggles. Married off shortly after college to a man she barely knew, she was grappling with cultural expectations that seemed at odds with her own desires. Our sessions became a safe space for both of us—me, processing the seismic shift in my life, and her, quietly questioning the path laid out for her.

I lived in a kind of fantasy world back then, clinging to the belief that I'd recover in time for the prom. Kripa indulged in this dream, but with a gentle honesty that helped me slowly come to terms with my new reality. She had a way of supporting my hopes while also grounding me in what was realistic for my recovery.

Years later, when I returned to the Children's Hospital in Philadelphia, I learned that Kripa's life had taken its own dramatic turn. She had divorced her husband, came out as a lesbian to her parents back in India, then returned to America to go on with her new life. Her family's reaction had been difficult, leaving her relationship with them strained.

Seeing Kripa again was like watching a butterfly emerge from its chrysalis. Gone were the traditional Indian outfits, replaced by jeans and plaid shirts. Her hair was cut short, and there was a new glow about her—the unmistakable radiance of someone finally living their truth.

At that moment, I realized that our journeys, though different, shared a common thread. We had both faced life-altering events that forced us to confront who we really were and what we truly wanted from life. Kripa had found the courage to break free from societal expectations and embrace her authentic self, just as I had learned to redefine my identity in the wake of my accident.

Our reunion was a powerful reminder that healing comes in many forms. For me, it was learning to navigate the world with a disability. For Kripa, it was finding the strength to live openly and honestly. As we caught up on the years that had passed, I felt a deep sense of gratitude for the role Kripa had played in my recovery. She had been more than just a physical therapist; she had been a friend, a confidante, and an unwitting role model in the art of personal transformation.

In the end, our paths had diverged, but the impact of our time together remained. Kripa had helped me take my first steps towards a new life, and in doing so, had unknowingly taken steps towards her own transformation.

IN THE WAKE OF MY 'NEW NORMAL' after the accident, the walls of Hunter College began to feel confining, not just physically but emotionally. The constant presence of my mother, while well-intentioned, had begun to chafe against my growing desire for independence. It wasn't that I had completed my studies at Hunter; rather, I felt an urgent need to reclaim the autonomy I had lost. This yearning led me to make a bold decision: to transfer to Caldwell University in New Jersey.

The move wasn't about academic dissatisfaction or completing a program. It was about distance—both physical and psychological. I craved the kind of independence I had tasted during my boarding school days, a freedom that had been abruptly curtailed by my accident. The thought of being 22 and still living under my parents' watchful eyes while my sister was away at school in California felt suffocating.

Caldwell offered more than just a new academic environment; it presented an opportunity to redefine myself away from the constant reminders of my limitations and the trauma our family had endured. It was a chance to prove, primarily to myself, that my disability didn't have to dictate the boundaries of my world.

Naturally, my parents objected. Their nervousness was palpable and understandable. The last time they had allowed their children the freedom of being away at school, disaster had struck. My accident had not only changed my life but had changed our lives forever.

My sister's struggles added another layer of complexity to their concerns. Her diagnosis of bipolar disorder, possibly triggered or exacerbated by the trauma of my accident, was a constant reminder of how fragile our mental and emotional states could be. I remembered the times I had rushed to her high school, heart pounding, to help her through anxiety attacks. Now, she was across the country at Pomona College in California, perhaps seeking her own form of escape from our family's tumultuous history.

As I contemplated this move to Caldwell, I couldn't help but draw parallels between my sister's choice to study so far from home and my own desire for independence. Were we both, in our own ways, trying to distance ourselves from the heavy atmosphere that had settled over our family in the wake of my accident?

The decision to transfer to Caldwell wasn't made lightly. It was a delicate balance between honoring my family's concerns and asserting my need for growth and self-discovery. I knew that my choice would add to my parents' worries, but I also believed that it was a necessary step in my journey of recovery—not just physical, but emotional and psychological as well.

THIS MOVE REPRESENTED MORE than just a change of scenery or academic environment. It was about reclaiming my narrative, about proving to myself—and perhaps to my family—that I could navigate the world independently, despite my physical challenges. It was a statement that my accident had changed me, but it hadn't defeated me.

As I prepared for this new chapter at Caldwell, I carried with me a complex mix of emotions: excitement for the future, gratitude for my family's support, and a determination to honor the resilience that had brought me this far. The path ahead was uncertain, but I was ready to face it, one step at a time, embracing the independence I had once known and now yearned to reclaim.

I decided not to have a roommate while at Caldwell and this was more than just a preference for solitude. It was a shield, a way to protect myself from the vulnerability I wasn't ready to face. The thought of someone witnessing my daily struggles—the intricate dance of dressing one-handed, using my teeth to tie shoelaces, and navigating life with a leg brace—was terrifying. I was barely accepting these new realities myself; how could I possibly let someone else into that fragile space?

So, I built walls, carefully crafting an image of capability and strength for the outside world. On campus, I was the studious, attentive student leader, president of the Women in Business Organization for two years running. I wore the shoes I wanted, even if it meant sizing up to accommodate my brace. I pushed myself to meet deadlines without asking for the extra time my cognitive remedial therapist had recommended.

This determination to appear "normal" was a double-edged sword. On one hand, it drove me to excel, to prove to myself and others that my disability doesn't define me. On the other, it meant denying a part of myself, hiding the very real challenges I faced daily.

When professors would reach out, offering extra time for assignments, I'd politely decline. The moment a timer started on an exam, I'd begin writing furiously, determined to finish alongside my peers. For papers, I'd start researching immediately, pushing myself to meet deadlines without any special consideration.

Looking back, I can see how this behavior echoed my father's words from those early days of physical therapy: "You used to be a runner, let's keep it going, let's keep it moving till we're back running again." Those words had become more than just encouragement; they were a metaphor for how I approached life post-accident. There was no room for stopping, no space for acknowledging limitations or asking for help.

This relentless drive served me well in many ways. It pushed me to achieve things that others might have thought impossible given my circumstances. But it also came at a cost. By never allowing myself to be vulnerable, to accept help or accommodation, I was denying a fundamental part of my new reality.

The irony wasn't lost on me. In my efforts to prove I was just like everyone else, I was setting myself apart, creating a barrier between myself and potential connections. The very thing I feared—being seen as different—was exactly what I was reinforcing through my refusal to acknowledge my needs.

It's a pattern I've come to recognize over the years, this tension between wanting to be seen as capable and needing to accept help. Learning to find a balance between these two poles has been ongoing. But with time, I've learned that true strength isn't about hiding our vulnerabilities, but about having the courage to acknowledge them, to ask for help when needed, and to allow others to see us as we truly are—challenges, triumphs, and all.

Q'addriyah emerged as an unexpected beacon of friendship. We were an unlikely pair—me, grappling with the physical challenges of my disability, and her, battling the invisible demons of an eating disorder. Yet, in our differences, we found a profound connection.

Q'addriyah was strikingly tall and thin, her 5'9" frame carrying barely 120 pounds. Her struggle with body image was a silent battle, one that mirrored my own internal conflicts in many ways. We were both fighting to reconcile our outer appearances with our inner selves, though our challenges manifested in vastly different ways.

Our friendship blossomed effortlessly, untainted by the self-consciousness that often plagued me in the wake of my accident. For the first time since that life-altering event, I found myself in a relationship where my disability didn't define me. Q'addriyah never asked about my limp or my unused left arm. Some might view this as indifference, but to me, it was a gift—the freedom to simply be, without explanation or apology.

We leaned on each other, finding strength in our shared determination to overcome our individual obstacles. Our bond was cemented by coincidences that felt like cosmic alignment—our mothers' birthdays just a month apart, our lives intersecting in ways that seemed predestined.

This friendship became a transformative force in my life, boosting my confidence and challenging my fears about forming close relationships post-accident. It was a living testament to the fact that true connection transcends physical limitations and societal expectations.

Our shared drive extended to our academic pursuits. We pushed each other to excel, turning our personal challenges into fuel for our ambitions. I threw myself into my studies with a fervor that surprised even me. In just two years, I graduated with honors, completing three years' worth of coursework in half the time. My political science degree, with a minor in business management, was hard-earned, each grade a battle won against the limitations others might have imposed on me.

Graduating cum laude with a 3.8 GPA, without ever asking for the concessions I was entitled to, felt like a personal triumph. It was a statement to the world—and to myself—that my disability would not define the trajectory of my life.

As the years have passed, Q'addriyah and I have remained friends, our bond weathering the tests of time and distance. She's found her footing in the world of communications and PR, while I pursued my own path. We've both grown, changed, and healed in our own ways. Q'addriyah has found a healthier relationship with her body, and I've learned to navigate the world with more confidence.

LOOKING BACK, I'm struck by the power of this friendship. In Q'addriyah, I found not just a study partner or a confidante, but a mirror reflecting my own strength and resilience. Our friendship was a crucial chapter in my journey of self-acceptance, teaching me that connection doesn't require explanation or justification. It simply requires the courage to be authentically ourselves, imperfections and all.

CHAPTER 5

# Roots and Wings

THE SUMMER I TURNED 21, my family and I returned to Ghana for a visit. It was during this trip that I met Junior, a man who would become a significant part of my life for the next three years. Junior was everything I thought I wanted in a partner—tall, handsome, and completely able-bodied. OK, maybe his name could have used a little work. But he checked most of my boxes! More importantly, he seemed to see beyond my disability, treating me as a whole person rather than a collection of limitations.

Our relationship blossomed quickly; the intensity of our connection heightened by the knowledge that we'd soon be separated by an ocean. As I returned to the US to continue my studies at Caldwell, we embarked on the challenging journey of long-distance love. Every break, every holiday became an opportunity to reunite in Ghana, our time together always feeling too short, too precious.

My parents, especially my father, were thrilled to see me in a relationship. I suspect they saw it as a sign of normalcy, a step towards the life they had envisioned for me before the accident. Their approval, while comforting, also added a layer of pressure to make the relationship work.

But as time went on, doubts began to creep in. There were moments, fleeting at first but growing more frequent, when I questioned Junior's intentions. It wasn't anything overt, just a nagging feeling that something wasn't quite right.

The first time I felt this unease was when I overheard a conversation between Junior and his friends. They were joking, their voices low but not low enough, about how Junior should "get her to buy you a ticket to the US." The words stung, not just because of their implication, but because Junior didn't immediately shut down such talk.

It was as if his friends couldn't conceive of the idea that someone like Junior—handsome, able-bodied, with his whole life ahead of him—could genuinely be interested in someone like me. In their eyes, there had to be an ulterior motive, a hidden agenda. And that agenda, apparently, was a ticket to America.

These moments of doubt became more frequent as our relationship progressed. I found myself constantly second-guessing Junior's actions, wondering if each gesture of affection was genuine or part of a long con. It was an exhausting way to live, always on guard, always analyzing.

Despite these reservations, our relationship lasted three years. From 2007 to 2010, Junior was a constant in my life. We weathered the challenges of long-distance romance, the cultural differences between Ghana and America, and the unspoken questions about our future.

During this time, I completed my degree at Caldwell, graduating in 2009 with a sense of accomplishment that was tempered by the uncertainty of my personal life. As I walked across the stage to receive my diploma, I couldn't help but wonder what Junior was thinking back in Ghana. Was he proud of me? Or was he simply biding his time, waiting for his opportunity to come to America?

There were moments when I seriously considered marrying Junior. After all, wasn't this what I had dreamed of? A relationship with someone who saw me for who I was, who wasn't deterred by my disability? But each time I entertained the thought of marriage, those nagging doubts would resurface.

Looking back, I realize that my relationship with Junior was as much about my own insecurities as it was about his potential ulterior motives. I was so eager to be seen as "normal," to have a relationship that mirrored what I thought love should look like, that I was willing to overlook red flags.

The stark difference in our physical appearances—him standing tall at 6 feet, the picture of health and vitality, and me with my visible disability—often drew curious glances from strangers. While part of me reveled in defying their expectations, another part wondered if they were right to be skeptical.

In the end, our relationship couldn't withstand the weight of these doubts and uncertainties. However, it taught me valuable lessons about self-worth, the importance of trusting my instincts, and the complexities of navigating relationships with a disability.

My time with Junior was a crucial chapter in my journey of self-discovery. It forced me to confront my own biases and insecurities, to question what I truly wanted in a partner, and to realize that being seen beyond my disability wasn't enough—I needed to be valued for all that I am, my limitations, and my strengths alike.

The complexities of my relationship with Junior deepened as my family became more involved. What had started as a personal connection soon became entangled with family expectations and, unbeknownst to me at the time, my father's own hidden agenda.

When Junior and I first met, he was working in his family's store, having paused his education after high school. My parents, especially my father, saw potential in his situation. Looking back, I realize they approached him with a combination of genuine concern and hope, though it carried expectations I didn't fully understand at the time.

"Do you want to be with my daughter?" my father asked Junior, his tone implying that the correct answer would require more than just affection. In my family, education was paramount, a non-negotiable stepping stone to success and acceptance. It was clear that if Junior wanted a future with me, going back to school was a prerequisite.

Junior's response was honest, touching on a reality many face. "I want to go back to school, but financially, I can't right now," he admitted. His words resonated with me, reminding me of the privilege my own education represented.

It was then that my father suggested something that would alter the course of our relationship. He proposed that I support Junior's return to education using my funds. The idea was presented as a way to invest in our future together, a gesture that would strengthen our bond and align Junior with our family's values.

Eager to please and genuinely wanting to help Junior, I agreed. It felt like a tangible way to support the man I cared for, to give him the opportunity that circumstances had denied him. I saw it as an investment in our shared future, a way to bridge the gap between our backgrounds.

The years between 2006 and 2008/2009 became a blur of transatlantic flights and divided loyalties. My sister and I found ourselves frequently traveling to Ghana, our hearts pulled by the gravitational force of budding romances. I was there for Junior, and my sister for her own boyfriend, our visits becoming more frequent as our relationships deepened.

These trips, ostensibly about nurturing our romantic connections, were unknowingly facilitating a web of deception that would take years to fully unravel. I remember vividly one particular trip to the airport. My father, in an uncharacteristic display of permissiveness, not only booked a hotel room for himself but encouraged my sister and me to do the same with our boyfriends. At the time, it seemed like a gesture of trust, a recognition of our adulthood. Now, I understand it was a calculated move to create space for his own indiscretions.

Even the most liberal of parents would hesitate to explicitly encourage their daughters to share hotel rooms with boyfriends. But at the moment, blinded by love and the excitement of our visits, we didn't question it. We were too caught up in our own stories to see the subplot unfolding around us.

Against the backdrop of the difficulties made apparent in my relationship with my father, things with Junior, already strained by distance, began to unravel. Maintaining a connection across continents proved more difficult than we had anticipated. Trust, that delicate thread that binds long-distance relationships, began to fray.

Then came the blow that shattered whatever illusions remained. Junior had cheated, and not only that, but the other woman was pregnant. The news hit me like a physical force, leaving me reeling. All the sacrifices, the money sent for his education, the emotional investment—it all seemed to crumble in an instant.

Yet, even as my romantic relationship disintegrated, it opened a channel for truths I had been blind to. After our breakup, Junior began to share snippets of information about my father's behavior. These revelations aligned with suspicions that had been growing in my mind.

Slowly, my father's motivations began to surface, revealing a web of deceit I hadn't imagined possible. What I had believed to be paternal concern for my relationship and Junior's future was, in fact, a carefully constructed facade hiding my father's own indiscretions.

The truth, when it finally came to light, was devastating. My father had been using his trips to Ghana, ostensibly to check on Junior's progress and our relationship, as cover for his own affairs. He had befriended Junior and another young man, a friend of my cousin's, effectively buying their silence about his Ghanaian girlfriend.

The realization that my father had manipulated not just me but also Junior and our relationship for his own ends was a bitter pill to swallow. It cast a shadow over every interaction, every piece of advice he had given. The man I had looked up to, the father who had stood by me through my recovery, suddenly appeared as a stranger, capable of deep deception.

This revelation forced me to re-evaluate not just my relationship with Junior, but also my understanding of family, trust, and the motivations behind seemingly selfless actions. I found myself questioning every decision and every piece of advice I had followed. Had my support of Junior's education truly been for our benefit, or was it just another pawn in my father's complex game of deception?

The pain of this betrayal was compounded by the realization that Junior had been complicit in keeping my father's secret. Whether out of loyalty, fear, or hope for continued financial support, he had chosen to remain silent about my father's infidelity. This silence spoke volumes about the foundation of trust—or lack thereof—in our relationship.

As I grappled with these revelations, I felt a profound sense of loss. Not just of the relationship I thought I had with Junior, but of the image I held of my father and even of my own judgment. How could I have been so blind to the manipulations happening around me?

I remembered times when I had sent money to my father for Junior's tuition, only to have Junior report back that he had received only a portion of it, or sometimes nothing at all. I had brushed these discrepancies aside at the time, unable or unwilling to confront the implications. Now, they took on a sinister new light.

The long-distance nature of our relationship, which had seemed romantic at first, became a breeding ground for deceit. The space between us, meant to be bridged by trust and communication, instead became filled with secrets and lies. It wasn't just Junior's infidelity; it was as if the very air of Ghana had become thick with unspoken truths and hidden agendas.

As I pieced together the fragments of truth from Junior's revelations and my own memories, a picture emerged of my father that was far from the one I had held dear. The man who had supported me through my recovery, who had encouraged my independence and education, was also capable of deep betrayal.

The realization was devastating. It felt as if the ground beneath my feet, already unstable from my accident and recovery, was shifting once again. The pillars of trust and family that I had leaned on were revealed to be as fragile as spun glass.

Yet, in the midst of this turmoil, I found an unexpected strength. The very resilience that had carried me through my physical recovery now became my emotional armor. I realized that while I couldn't control the actions of others, I could control my response to them.

This chapter of my life, painful as it was, became a crucible for personal growth. It taught me the importance of maintaining my own identity and values, even in the face of familial expectations and manipulations. It reinforced the need for clear boundaries and open communication in all relationships, romantic or familial.

Most importantly, it reminded me that my worth was not determined by my ability to please others or conform to their expectations. My journey forward would be on my own terms, guided by my own moral compass, not by the hidden agendas of others.

As I looked back on those years of frequent trips to Ghana, of love and betrayal, of hidden truths and painful revelations, I realized that they had shaped me in ways I was only beginning to understand. They taught me about the complexities of human nature, about the capacity for both love and deceit that exists in all of us. Life is full of gray areas and the dichotomy of black and white is a thing for storybooks.

These experiences reinforced the value of self-reliance and self-truth. In a world where even those closest to us can betray our trust, the ability to stand firm in our own convictions becomes paramount.

## CHAPTER 6

# *Ancient Wisdom*

IN 2006, I FOUND MYSELF returning to Ghana for the first time since my family had left in the mid-90s. It was a journey laden with anticipation and unspoken expectations. This homecoming carried the weight of family history and cultural beliefs I was only beginning to understand and wasn't sure I could uphold.

Two and a half years had passed since my accident and the scars, visible and invisible, were still fresh. My maternal grandmother had been imploring my mother to bring her granddaughters back to Ghana. There was an urgency in her request. It was as if she sensed that her time in this world was drawing to a close. Her desire to see us one last time was a poignant reminder of the connections that endure despite time and distance.

My parents, ever hopeful for my full recovery, were keen to explore the traditional medicine options in Ghana. Their interest wasn't merely born out of desperation but of deep-seated faith in the healing powers of our ancestral land. It was a belief that sometimes clashed with my Westernized perspective, yet I couldn't deny the pull of these ancient practices.

As we settled into life in Ghana, I became acutely aware of the cultural beliefs surrounding my condition. Many Ghanaians, steeped in traditional beliefs, viewed my accident through a lens of karmic retribution. The whispers of whether I had done something in a past life to deserve such a fate were subtle but unmistakable. It was a perspective that both fascinated and unsettled me and these instincts forced me to confront the complex tapestry of beliefs that made up my heritage.

The duality of faith in Ghana never ceased to amaze me. On one hand, Christianity pervaded every aspect of life but, on the other, traditional beliefs held sway over many people's actions. This made me think of my nanny who would take herbal remedies before considering a trip to the hospital. The blend of the modern and the traditional was a constant reminder of the intricate cultural landscape I was navigating.

Family dynamics added another layer of complexity to our visit. My father's mother, a woman I had met only twice in my life, had never truly accepted my mother into her family. The fact that my father was half-Caucasian seemed to be at the root of this discord. In my father's mother's eyes, my mother had taken her son away and this perceived slight had soured our relationship before it even had a chance to form.

The absence of my paternal grandfather loomed large in our family narrative. He was a Scottish man who had returned to his other family and left his Ghanaian connections behind. He was more of a myth than a real person to me, but his influence was undeniable. As I walked the streets of Ghana, people would often remark on my resemblance to other Pattersons in the area. It seemed that my grandfather had left more than just memories behind by planting seeds across Ghana before returning to Scotland.

With paternal grandmother while doing treatment in Ghana

Although my father's story was one of success, it was also tinged with abandonment. As a bank manager, he had been the most successful of his siblings (a fact that only added to the bitterness of his departure). I couldn't help but wonder about the lives he had touched, and perhaps altered, during his time in Ghana.

Amidst these family dynamics, deeper cultural beliefs began to surface. There were quiet conversations about witchcraft and black magic, with some wondering if my paternal grandmother's strained relationship with my mother might have played a part in my misfortune. These reflections highlighted the enduring influence of traditional beliefs in the supernatural that remain present in parts of Ghana.

As I grappled with these swirling emotions and cultural complexities, my maternal grandmother's reaction to my condition stood out in stark contrast. Upon our return in 2006, she behaved as if nothing had happened to me. Her denial was both baffling and oddly comforting. It was hard to tell whether she was simply refusing to acknowledge my changed circumstances or if she had some stubborn belief in my inherent wholeness despite my physical limitations.

The belief in the power of spirits to influence our earthly lives runs deep in Ghana. It's not just a fringe idea, but a core belief for many that shapes their understanding of fortune and misfortune alike. The belief that otherworldly forces are able to bring about good or bad in our lives was something I found both fascinating and unsettling.

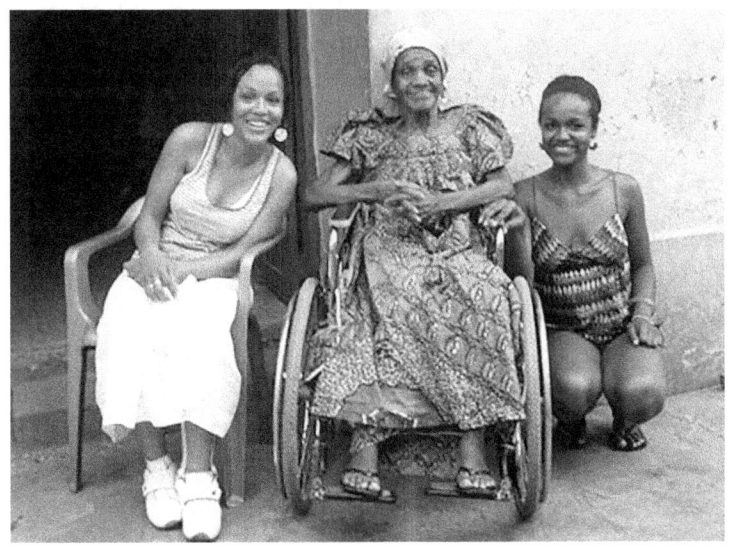

My grandmother and sister with me in leg brace

I spent several months exploring traditional medicine with my mother in Ghana in the hopes that there was some potential aid for my arm. It was a journey into a world far removed from the sterile hospitals and rehabilitation centers that I had become accustomed to in the States. An herbalist became a regular visitor to our house and his presence marked the rhythm of our days.

Twice daily, morning and evening, he would arrive with his arsenal of herbs that all had their own purported healing properties. The concoctions he mixed were complex and their scents were pungent and earthy. As he applied these mixtures to my arm, I couldn't help but wonder about the ancient knowledge that informed his practice. Was there wisdom here that modern medicine had overlooked, or was this simply the placebo effect of hope and tradition?

The treatments didn't stop at topical applications. I was instructed to participate in steam treatments that involved covering my head in cloth as I inhaled the fumes of the herbs. The steam would envelop me and, in those moments, wrapped in warmth and the heady scent of unfamiliar plants, I felt as though I was suspended between two worlds—the Ghana of my heritage and the America of my upbringing.

It was during this time that my Aunt Agnes, my mother's older sister, invited us to her church to see her pastor. This invitation came with an air of secrecy and my mother made it clear that my father was not to know about this visit. His skepticism towards such practices was a well-known point of contention in their relationship that I was only beginning to fully understand.

The church visit was unlike anything I had experienced before. As we entered the pastor's house, we were greeted by a group gathered for prayers. The atmosphere was charged with anticipation and faith. We were all instructed to stand and I felt a surge of energy in the room as the chanting prayers began.

Soon, the pastor approached me. His eyes were intense with purpose and what happened next was both terrifying and surreal. He attempted to exorcize what he believed was a devil inside me. His voice rose in fervent prayer as I stood there, a mix of confusion and awe washing over me. Was there really something inside me that needed to be cast out or was this simply another way of trying to make sense of my condition?

As the pastor moved on, the lady next to me suddenly spasmed and fell to the floor. The visceral demonstration of faith's power, or perhaps something more, was nothing like I had ever seen. I couldn't help but wonder if she truly felt something I couldn't or if the intensity of the moment had simply overwhelmed her.

When the pastor returned to me, his second attempt at exorcism was met with the same result as the first—nothing. I stood there, unchanged, as he declared once again that there was nothing inside me. At that moment, I felt a strange mix of relief and disappointment. I was relieved to not experience the same violent reaction as the woman next to me but disappointed that this, too, seemed to be another dead end in my search for healing.

As we left the church that day, I was struck by the complexity of faith and healing in Ghana. The herbalist and his ancient remedies and the pastor's fervent prayers represented different facets of a culture striving to make sense of illness and misfortune. It left me straddling two worlds as I tried to reconcile the scientific explanations I had been given in America with the spiritual and traditional approaches of my ancestral home.

This experience left me with more questions than answers. It challenged my understanding of healing, faith, and the unseen forces that many believe shape our lives. While I couldn't fully embrace these beliefs, I couldn't dismiss them either. They were part of my heritage and a reminder of the complex tapestry of culture and tradition that had shaped my family long before my accident.

After a year of exploring traditional remedies and spiritual interventions in Ghana my mother and I finally conceded that our quest for herbal medicine had reached its end. In 2007, with a mixture of resignation and hope, we packed our bags and returned to New York where my father and sister had been waiting for us.

The year in Ghana had been an eye-opening experience, not just in terms of alternative healing methods, but also in confronting the cultural attitudes towards disability. I remember vividly one Sunday when I attended church wearing a leg brace and a dress. The disapproving whispers and sidelong glances culminated in someone boldly asking my mother, "How could you bring her here wearing this?" The words stung and revealed a deep-seated stigma that I hadn't fully grasped before. It was a stark reminder that, in some parts of the Ghanaian culture, people with disabilities are often hidden away as if their very existence was something to be ashamed of.

This experience was further underscored by my interactions with Farida Bedwei, a woman I met at a TED Talk in Accra. Farida was born with cerebral palsy and we are mistaken for one another, despite looking nothing alike. Our only commonalities were our light skin and our disabilities. To many, our surface-level similarities were enough to render us interchangeable, and our individual identities were often overshadowed by our physical conditions. But while those comparisons lingered, my journey took its own distinct path.

After years of healing and hard work, I returned to New York, ready to reclaim pieces of the life I had once envisioned for myself. Enrolling at Caldwell University became a pivotal step in that process. Determined to make up for lost time, I immersed myself in my studies, embracing both the challenges and opportunities that came my way. In 2009, I proudly walked across the stage to receive my degree—a moment that stood as a testament to my perseverance and the unwavering support of my family.

It wasn't until several years later, in 2015, that I met Farida. By then, I had already carved out a new chapter in my life, one that continued to evolve in ways I hadn't imagined.

With my degree in hand, I embarked on a new chapter as a teacher at the Cornelia Connelly Center for Girls Education on the Lower East Side. Co-teaching English and social studies while taking religion classes on my own was challenging but rewarding. The two-year interim position seemed like the perfect opportunity to make a difference in young lives.

However, the realities of the job soon tested my resolve. The school provided housing, but it was on the fifth floor of a building with an unreliable elevator. Each day was a physical challenge that only reminded me of the limitations I was still learning to navigate. The constant struggle to reach my apartment wore on me, both physically and emotionally.

My role extended beyond the classroom, as I also served as a high school admissions counselor. Many of the girls came from low-income backgrounds. They were bright minds plucked from public schools for this opportunity. It was a system reminiscent of a charter school by identifying promising students and offering them a chance at a better education.

Working with these girls was both inspiring and heartbreaking. I saw myself in their determination and their hunger for knowledge and opportunity. I also saw the harsh realities of their lives and the obstacles they faced that went far beyond academics. Some days, navigating the complex web of socioeconomic challenges that affected my students' lives made me feel more like a social worker than a teacher.

As the months wore on, the physical toll of the job, combined with the emotional weight of my students' struggles, chipped away at my spirit. I found myself questioning whether I could sustain this pace and if my body could keep up with the demands of my chosen profession. The irony wasn't lost on me. I was trying to empower these young women to overcome their circumstances, all while barely grappling with my own limitations.

In the end, I didn't complete the full two years of my contract. The decision to leave was difficult and fraught with feelings of guilt and disappointment, but it was also a moment of growth. I recognized that acknowledging my limits wasn't a sign of weakness, but a necessary step in my ongoing journey of self-discovery and adaptation.

As I packed up my classroom, I reflected on the lessons I'd learned. I had pushed my boundaries, faced my limitations head-on, and, in the process, gained a deeper understanding of what I was capable of. More importantly, I touched the lives of my students by inspiring them to see beyond their own perceived limitations, just as I was learning to do.

After leaving my teaching position, I found myself at a crossroads. I searched for a new direction that would align with my passions and accommodate my physical realities. I saw that the Council of Urban Professionals (CUP) was offering an internship and I found myself drawn to the position. The organization's focus on supporting minority professionals resonated with my own experiences and aspirations. I threw myself into the work, eager to contribute to their mission, and assisted with various tasks and projects.

However, the environment at CUP proved to be more challenging than I had anticipated. The fast-paced, high-pressure atmosphere began to take its toll. The demands of the job exposed limitations I hadn't fully recognized before and pushed me to confront the ongoing impact of my accident in new ways.

One morning, as I made my way to catch the bus to work, the world around me suddenly blurred. Street signs became indecipherable smudges and the buses passing by were nothing more than vague, moving shapes. The sudden loss of visual clarity was a stark reminder of how fragile recovery could be.

This incident forced me to acknowledge a truth I had been reluctant to face. My vision, which had always been good before the accident, had been affected more than I'd realized. The intense exposure to screens in my work environment had exacerbated the issue so much that it was affecting my day-to-day. When I finally got glasses, it felt like a tangible byproduct of the accident. They were a visible reminder of how that event continued to shape my life in unexpected ways.

The experience at CUP, and the subsequent vision issues, served as a wake-up call. I realized that I needed to reassess my path and find a way forward that would allow me to pursue my goals without compromising my health. It was in this moment of reflection that the idea of graduate school began to take shape.

With a mixture of hope and trepidation, I began the application process. I applied to seven schools and each application felt like a step toward a new chapter in my life. The New School offered me a half scholarship and I regained the confidence that I lost after my accident. One by one, acceptance letters arrived and affirmed that my dreams were within reach. The only detour in my yellow brick road was my letter from NYU Wagner Graduate Center of Public Service which stated I was waitlisted. This was a small disappointment in an otherwise encouraging process.

As I weighed my options, NYU continued to linger in my mind. Despite being waitlisted, something about the school called to me. Perhaps it was the idea of proving myself in a program that had initially hesitated to accept me, or maybe it was the school's reputation and the opportunities it could offer. Whatever the reason, when the chance to attend NYU for my master's degree finally presented itself, I seized it without hesitation.

In 2011, I stepped onto the NYU campus filled with a

mix of excitement and apprehension. This new beginning represented more than just an educational opportunity. It was a chance to redefine myself once again and push beyond the limitations—both real and perceived—that had accumulated since my accident.

The journey to this point had been far from straightforward. Each setback—from the challenges of teaching to the struggles at CUP to the unexpected vision issues—had served as a stepping stone that guided me toward this moment. As I navigated the bustling NYU campus, I couldn't help but reflect on the winding path that had brought me here.

Graduate school presented its own set of challenges. The academic rigor was intense and demanded a level of focus and dedication that pushed me to my limits. But there was also a sense of liberation in being back in an academic environment. Here, my ideas and intellect took center stage and offered a respite from the constant awareness of the physical limitations that had dominated my professional experiences.

As I immersed myself in my studies, I found my worldview expanding. The diverse perspectives of my classmates, the challenging discussions in seminars, and the exposure to new ideas all contributed to my intellectual growth. The walls that had seemed to close in around me in my previous roles were now expanding and revealing new possibilities and potential paths forward.

Yet, even as I embraced this new chapter, I remained acutely aware of the journey that had brought me here. Each lecture I attended and paper I wrote was infused with the perspective gained through my accident, recovery, and struggles in the workplace. These weren't just academic exercises but opportunities to synthesize my lived experiences with new knowledge and create a unique lens through which to view the world.

As I progressed through my NYU program, I began to see how my past experiences, even the most challenging ones, were profoundly shaping my academic journey. The resilience I had developed and the adaptability I had been forced to cultivate now served me well in the demanding graduate environment. My unique perspective, born from overcoming obstacles many of my peers couldn't imagine, added depth to class discussions and brought a different dimension to group projects.

The curriculum was rigorous and challenged me intellectually in ways I hadn't experienced before. Courses in financial management, microeconomics, and public policy opened my eyes to the complex systems that govern our society and the potential for change within them.

Yet, the path to graduation was far from smooth. I faced a devastating setback when I failed two classes in my first semester and my confidence received a staggering blow. The administration suggested I transfer to another school and the recommendation felt like a death knell to my ambitions. At that moment, I felt the weight of every obstacle I'd overcome since my accident bearing down on me. However, the same resilience that had carried me through my physical recovery began fueling my determination to stay at NYU.

I campaigned fiercely to remain in the program. My tears and pleas were a testament to how much this opportunity meant to me. This was more than just a degree to me; it was a chance to prove to myself and others that my disability doesn't define my capabilities. Eventually, my persistence paid off and I was allowed to continue my studies.

During this time, I was also working part-time remotely for Junior Achievement New York, JA- New York. However, as the demands of my coursework increased, I made the difficult decision to quit and focus entirely on my studies. It was a risk, but one I felt was necessary to achieve my academic goals.

As I closed this chapter of my life, I couldn't help but marvel at the journey that had brought me here. From the herbalist's house in Ghana to being about to partake in the bustling campus of NYU, each step had been a lesson in resilience and adaptability.

But as I stood on the cusp of a new beginning, I knew the real challenge was yet to come. Manhattan beckoned, promising independence and opportunity in equal measure. How would I navigate this concrete jungle, both physically and emotionally? Could I carve out a life for myself, away from the safety net of family and familiar surroundings?

As I packed my bags for this new adventure, a mix of excitement and trepidation coursed through me. Little did I know, I would be tested in ways I couldn't imagine, pushing me to redefine not just my capabilities, but my very identity.

# CHAPTER 7

# Love's Lessons

AMIDST THE INTENSITY OF GRADUATE SCHOOL, I took another leap toward independence and rented a studio apartment in Manhattan. This small space soon became my sanctuary. It was a place away from the well-meaning, but sometimes stifling, care of my family and where I could fully gain control over my autonomy.

During this period of newfound independence, I met Brandon at the Roots Picnic, a hip-hop festival in Philadelphia. Our meeting was serendipitous. He traveled to the East Coast from Nevada for the concert. Despite the brief encounter, our connection was immediate and intense and we took a cab together back to NYC and began dating shortly after. The day I met Brandon, I was with my friend Charlene in the park. Initially, I assumed he was interested in Charlene—after all, who would want to talk to me? But, throughout the day, Brandon found ways to be near me and his interest became unmistakable and flattering.

Brandon was unlike anyone I had dated before. He had a decidedly nerdy air about him. He was tall, and skinny, wore glasses, and had a background in mathematics. He had originally planned to go into engineering, a path that would have pleased his lawyer stepfather, but Brandon had chosen to follow his passion and dropped out of school to focus on music full-time. This decision disappointed his family but spoke to his determination to forge his own path. As our relationship developed, I found myself drawn to Brandon's quiet intensity and his willingness to defy expectations. In many ways, his journey mirrored my own. Both of us were navigating paths that diverged from what others had envisioned for us and were driven by passions that others might not understand.

Our connection was a bright spot in the otherwise demanding landscape of my graduate studies. Brandon's presence in my life added a new dimension to my experience of independence. For the first time since my accident, I felt seen not as someone to be pitied or cared for, but as a woman with desires, ambitions, and a future full of possibilities.

As I balanced the rigors of my academic life with the blossoming of this new relationship, I found myself reevaluating my perceptions of what was possible in my life. The girl who had once believed no one would be interested in her was now navigating a romance alongside her studies and her journey toward a fulfilling career.

Brandon's world was so different from mine, yet we found common ground in our shared love of music. Music is a source of joy for me and has always been a passion of mine. He was a violinist and street performer. His talent, raw and unrestrained, was a stark contrast to my more structured background. As a Black American, his cultural experiences were vastly different from my Ghanaian upbringing. At 26 or 27, I was still navigating the complexities of my identity and our relationship added another layer to that exploration.

For two years, we danced in and out of each other's lives. Brandon would visit me often in NYC and his presence was always a welcome respite from the demands of my graduate studies and the lingering challenges of my disability. Our time together was filled with music, laughter, and the kind of deep conversations that make you feel truly seen. But, as my time in New York drew to a close and my plans to return to Ghana solidified, the cracks in our relationship began to show. When I broached the subject of my impending move, Brandon's response was both comical and heartbreaking.

"I can't live in Africa," he declared, his voice tinged with genuine fear. "I don't want to be eaten or killed by mosquitos." His words, though partly in jest, exposed a deep gulf between us.

Despite the looming end of our relationship, I found myself visiting Brandon's family for Christmas. It was a bittersweet experience. His mother welcomed me with open arms and her warmth and acceptance only highlighted the growing distance I felt from Brandon. As we went through the motions of holiday celebrations, I could sense that Brandon had already made up his mind. Our relationship was over, even if the words hadn't been spoken yet. The irony wasn't lost on me—I was finally feeling accepted by a partner's family, only to have that acceptance potentially scare Brandon away. His mother's love for me brought a level of authenticity to our relationship that Brandon wasn't ready to embrace.

When the breakup finally came, the pain was intense but mercifully brief. For three days, I was devastated and it felt as if my world tilted on its axis. After my relationship with Junior, Brandon had been the first person to make me feel truly loved and accepted. The loss of that connection hit me hard and reopened wounds I thought had long since healed. But, as I had learned time and time again since my accident, resilience was my constant companion. After those three days of grief, I looked forward and turned my gaze toward Ghana and the next chapter of my life.

The decision to move back to Ghana came swiftly on the heels of my breakup with Brandon. It felt like closing a chapter, not just on our relationship, but on this entire phase of my life in America. As I packed my belongings, each item a reminder of the experiences I'd had and the person I'd become, I realized that my time with Brandon had taught me valuable lessons about love, acceptance, and the importance of cultural understanding in relationships. It showed me that I was capable of being loved, disability and all, and that my fears of never finding a connection were unfounded. As I prepared for my return to Ghana, I carried with me not just the memories of my time with Brandon, but a newfound confidence in myself and my ability to navigate complex emotional terrain. The girl who had once thought no one would want her had experienced love, loss, and everything in between.

MY IMPENDING MOVE TO GHANA represented more than just a geographical shift. It was a return to my roots, armed with the experiences and knowledge I'd gained during my time in America. The challenges I'd faced—from my accident to my academic struggles to my romantic entanglements—had all shaped me into the woman I was becoming. As I boarded the plane back to Ghana, I felt a mix of excitement and trepidation. I was leaving behind the familiar streets of New York, the academic halls of NYU, and the memories of my time with Brandon, but I was also moving towards something new and uniquely my own.

Ghana marked the beginning of a new chapter filled with unexpected turns and profound personal growth. With my father leading the way, my family had already established themselves there. I arrived with a sense of purpose and was determined to found an organization that would make a difference in the lives of young girls—the Girls Education Initiative of Ghana. As I threw myself into this new venture, my mother, ever the matchmaker, introduced me to Francis, an accountant she deemed suitable. At first, I welcomed his attention and found him a pleasant distraction from the pressures of starting a new organization. Francis was kind, stable, and genuinely interested in me. His desire to marry me was flattering, a balm to the lingering hurt from my breakup with Brandon.

However, Francis's interest soon took on an unsettling intensity. What had started as a welcome distraction quickly morphed into obsession. His constant presence and unwavering focus on our potential future together began to feel suffocating. It was a stark reminder that the path to finding genuine connection was rarely straightforward.

The potential of me having normal relations with the opposite sex, though exciting, also made me anxious. I am reminded of an encounter on a bus in New York that would stick with me for years. A man, after getting my number, boldly asked if I was able to have sex. His question, likely stemming from ignorance about my disability, sparked a fire in me.

"It was a brain injury," I retorted, my voice laced with a mixture of frustration and dark humor. "My vagina isn't broken." The incident, though brief, highlighted the misconceptions many held about individuals with disabilities and our capacity for full, rich lives—including romantic and sexual relationships.

It was against this backdrop of misguided suitors and societal misconceptions that I met Andy. Our first encounter was at a conference where, seeing potential in this articulate young man, I handed him my business card. I had first noticed him teaching when he was just 19 and, initially, my interest was purely professional. I saw myself as a mentor who could guide this promising young man in his career. Andy stood out among his peers. His eloquence and poise were remarkable, especially for someone who hadn't traveled much outside Ghana. There was a maturity and worldliness about him that belied his young age and limited experiences. When Andy found a job in Kumasi, where my mother and I were living in a spacious five-bedroom house, I saw an opportunity to support his budding career. With my mother's blessing, I invited Andy to stay with us. He moved in that very day and what was meant to be a temporary arrangement stretched into a year-long cohabitation.

Our daily conversations at the dining room table became a fixture in my life. Slowly, almost imperceptibly, our relationship evolved. What started as a professional mentorship blossomed into a deep friendship and, eventually, something more. The transition was gradual. Each day brought us closer and our understanding of each other deepened with every shared meal and late-night discussion. Yet, I was acutely aware of the complexities of our situation. At 28, I was not only older than Andy but also his boss. The age difference, while not vast, felt significant given his youth. Moreover, the power dynamic of our professional relationship added another layer of complication. For a long time, I refused to entertain the idea of a romantic relationship with Andy and pushed aside any feelings that threatened to surface.

But life, I was learning, had a way of upending our carefully laid plans and firmly held beliefs. As our friendship deepened and our connection grew stronger, I found myself questioning the boundaries I had set. The young man I had initially seen as a mentee was revealing himself to be a partner intellectually, emotionally, and eventually, romantically. Our evolving relationship forced me to confront my own biases and fears. Was I ready to open myself up to love again, especially with someone younger? Could I reconcile the professional and personal aspects of our connection? And, perhaps most importantly, was I willing to risk my heart again, knowing the pain that could come with vulnerability?

As I grappled with these questions, I realized that my journey—from accident survivor to graduate student to nonprofit founder—had prepared me for this moment in ways I couldn't have anticipated. Each challenge I faced taught me to look beyond surface-level judgments and value genuine connection over societal expectations.

Andy, with his wisdom beyond his years and his unwavering support of my goals, was challenging me to grow in new ways. He saw me not as a woman with a disability or as a boss to be impressed, but as a complex person who was worthy of love.

As our relationship teetered on the brink of something more than friendship, I found myself at another crossroads. The path ahead was uncertain and fraught with potential complications, but it also held the promise of a partnership based on mutual respect, shared values, and a deep understanding of each other. As my professional life began to take shape in Ghana, my personal world was undergoing seismic shifts. The foundation of my family, which had always been a source of stability, began to crumble. My parents, whose relationship I had always seen as unshakeable, decided to separate. The impact of their split reverberated through every aspect of my life and created a new reality that I was ill-prepared to navigate.

At 26, I found myself living with my mother in the

five-bedroom house that had once been a symbol of our family's unity. The space that had once echoed with the sounds of a full family now felt cavernous and empty. My father, unable or unwilling to stay in the home he and my mother had built together, retreated to the United States and left a void that seemed impossible to fill. In the wake of his departure, my mother and I struggled to find our footing in a landscape that had suddenly shifted beneath our feet. The unspoken truth hung heavy in the air. My presence in the house was a comfort to my mother and a buffer against the loneliness that threatened to engulf her, but, at 26, living with my mother felt like a step backward and a compromise of the independence I had fought so hard to achieve.

My days fell into a monotonous rhythm—work and back, work and back. The outside world, with its potential for social connections and new experiences, faded into the background as I immersed myself in my work. It became an excuse to avoid confronting the painful realities of my family's disintegration. The tension between my parents was obvious, even from a distance. I found myself caught in the middle as a reluctant mediator in a conflict I barely understood. Each phone call and message felt like navigating a minefield. I was careful not to take sides and tried desperately to maintain some semblance of family unity.

It was in this tumultuous period that Andy became a

more permanent fixture in our lives. Once my father left, Andy moved into our home and filled the space with his youthful energy and optimism. His presence was a welcome distraction and a reminder that life could still hold joy and promise even in the darkest of times. Yet, as I grew closer to Andy, I couldn't help but notice the stark contrasts in our experiences. He was book smart and his mind was a repository of knowledge and ideas but, when it came to the practicalities of life and the complex dance of human relationships and emotions, he was still learning. In many ways, we were teaching each other. I showed him the nuances of adult life while he reminded me of the power of hope and new beginnings.

As the days stretched into weeks and months, the weight of living with my mother began to take its toll. Her refusal to acknowledge the reality of my father's departure created a surreal atmosphere in the house. It was as if we were actors playing the part of a whole, happy family and pretending that the empty chair at the dinner table was just a temporary absence.

Watching my mother struggle to build her own identity outside of her role as my father's wife was both painful and enlightening. It forced me to confront my own fears about independence and self-identity. I began to realize that staying in that house, comforting as it might be for my mother, was stunting my own growth and healing.

The decision to move out was not an easy one, but it felt necessary for my sanity and personal development. I rented an apartment in Accra, a space that was entirely my own and free from the ghosts of my family's past and the weight of unspoken tensions. This move was more than just a change of address; it was a declaration of independence and a step towards creating my own life on my own terms. However, life had one more lesson in store for me. Shortly after moving into my new apartment, I was robbed. The violation of my new sanctuary shook me to my core and challenged my newfound sense of independence. But rather than retreating, I chose to see it as an opportunity for growth. I moved again, this time to a house that I bought as a tangible symbol of my resilience and determination to forge my path.

This period of my life, marked by family upheaval, personal growth, and the blossoming of a new relationship, taught me invaluable lessons about resilience, independence, and the complexities of human relationships. As I stood in my new home, I realized that each challenge—from my accident to my family's dissolution to this latest setback—had only served to make me stronger, more determined, and more aware of my capacity for growth and change.

As I settled into my new life in Ghana, I quickly realized that my circumstances set me apart from other young Ghanaian women. The fact that I had a driver and a car was unusual and didn't go unnoticed. When I moved into my apartment, my driver lived with me and the situation raised eyebrows and fueled speculation about my wealth. The perception of affluence became even more pronounced when my sister visited around Christmas time. To outsiders, we appeared to be rich American girls even though this was far from the truth. Little did we know, our presence had caught the attention of those with less than honorable intentions.

At the time, Ghana was in the grip of a severe power crisis. Each night, I would go to bed with my laptop and phones completely drained, desperately hoping they would charge during the sporadic moments of electricity. It was during one of these nights that my sense of security was shattered.

I woke with a start, an inexplicable feeling of unease washing over me. As my eyes adjusted to the darkness, I saw something that made my blood run cold—a hand reaching through the window, grasping for my electronics. Despite the security bars on the windows, someone had managed to pry them open and cut through the netting.

My scream pierced the night and jolted my sister and driver awake. In the early hours of the morning, around 3 or 4 a.m. we found ourselves at the police station to report the attempted theft. The police's nonchalant response, asking for a pencil rather than taking immediate action, was both frustrating and disheartening. We later learned that several apartments in the area had been targeted. Shaken by the incident, we retreated to my mother's house for the remainder of the holidays. It was during this time that I began searching for a more secure place to live. With my mother's help, I found a four-bedroom house and made a down payment.

My move to this new house in Accra marked a definitive break from living with my mother. It was a necessary step for my independence, but it also opened the door to new complexities in my life. Around this time, Andy, who had been living with his uncle and cousins, found himself in need of a place to stay. He had left his civil engineering studies out of boredom and taught himself coding so that he could build websites on contract. When his uncle expressed disapproval of his career change, Andy asked if he could rent a room in my new house.

Initially, our living arrangement was straightforward—Andy as a tenant, me as the homeowner. But, after a few months of seeing his financial struggles, I told him he could stay for free if he contributed to the utilities. This decision, made from kindness and practicality, unknowingly set the stage for a profound shift in our relationship. As we shared the same living space, Andy and I grew closer. Our daily interactions, shared meals, and late-night conversations fostered a deep connection. Then, one day, Andy confessed that he thought he was in love with me. His words sent me into a panic. The age difference, our professional relationship, and the potential complications all swirled in my mind.

Unsure how to proceed, I turned to my mother for advice. Her response was simple: "Pray about it." Reflecting through deep-rooted spirituality is a Ghanaian instinct that often guides decision-making in our culture. For about a year, Andy and I dated in secret. We navigated the complexities of our evolving relationship behind closed doors and away from the potential disapproval we might face. However, our secret was eventually discovered when my sister woke up one morning to find Andy not sleeping on the couch where he was supposed to be. While she liked Andy as a person, she was vehemently opposed to our romantic involvement.

The situation became even more complicated when, during a trip to the US, I discovered I was pregnant. This news added a new layer of urgency and complexity to our relationship. The traditional steps towards marriage never fully materialized due, in part, to my mother's protective stance regarding my assets. She insisted on a prenuptial agreement, but I struggled to accept the idea. In the eyes of our families and according to traditional customs, we were considered married.

There was an exchange of items between our families and a ceremony where it was declared, "If you're looking for your daughter, she is with me," but we never stood before an official to formalize our union legally.

This unconventional path to partnership, fraught with cultural expectations, family dynamics, and personal hesitations, ultimately led to our separation. The journey from mentor and mentee to partners and co-parents was a complex one, challenging my perceptions of love, commitment, and cultural norms. But little did I know, this was just the beginning of my adventure in defying expectations.

As a woman with a disability, society had long tried to dictate what I could and couldn't do. Parenthood, in many people's eyes, was supposed to be beyond my reach. Yet here I was, just a mother, ready to rewrite the rules of parenting as I knew them.

The road ahead would be filled with obstacles, judgments, and moments of self-doubt. But it would also be paved with triumphs, joy, and revelations that would shake the very foundation of what it means to be a parent in today's world. As I stood on the precipice of this new chapter, I couldn't help but wonder: How would my journey as a disabled mother challenge not just my own preconceptions, but those of everyone around me? And more importantly, how would it reshape the narrative for others who dared to dream beyond the boundaries society had set for them? Little did I know, the answers to these questions would come in ways I never could have imagined.

# CHAPTER 8

# Motherhood Without Maps

As I cradled my newborn son in my arms, the reality of motherhood began to sink in. It was a joy I had once feared might be beyond my reach, given my physical limitations, but here I was, a new mother, ready to take on the world. My own mother, ever-present and eager to help, suggested she take my baby and live in Kumasi. Her intentions were pure and born from a desire to ease my burden but, as I looked down at my son's tiny face, I felt a fierce protectiveness wash over me.

"Why would I let you do that and take this experience away from me?" I asked her, my voice soft but resolute. It wasn't that I didn't appreciate her offer, but I had fought so hard for my independence and had overcome so many obstacles to reach this point that the thought of relinquishing this precious time with my child, of missing out on the small, everyday moments of his growth, was unthinkable.

Instead, we compromised. I told her she could stay with me in Ghana for two weeks but, after that, I would look for a nanny. It was a decision that balanced my need for support with my desire for autonomy.

From the beginning, I was determined to be as hands-on a parent as possible. It wasn't just about proving to others that I could do it, but rather proving it to myself. Each diaper change and each feeding was a small victory and a testament to my capabilities. I remember one particular day when my son was just a few days old. My mother, ever-vigilant, had been by my side constantly.

"Take a nap while the baby is sleeping," she urged, her face etched with concern for my well-being. But, as I lay there, trying to rest, I heard my son stir. He had soiled his diaper. Without hesitation, I rose to tend to him. As I changed his diaper with one hand, a task that would have seemed impossible not long ago, I felt a surge of pride and accomplishment. At that moment, I realized that I could do it. I could be the mother I wanted to be, disability and all. From that day forward, I became even more protective of my time with my children. It wasn't that I didn't appreciate help, I just wanted to savor every moment and fully experience every aspect of motherhood. I wanted each milestone, each challenge, and each tender moment all for myself.

This desire to be fully present in my children's lives wasn't just about proving my capabilities, but also embracing a role I had once feared might be denied to me. Every sleepless night and every exhausting day was a gift and a reminder of how far I had come and the obstacles I had jumped. As I navigated the early days of motherhood, I found strength that I didn't know I possessed. The same determination that had carried me through my recovery now fueled my parenting. Yes, there were challenges and moments of frustration and exhaustion, but there was also joy—pure, unadulterated joy.

I learned to adapt and find creative solutions to the physical challenges I faced. Changing diapers became a one-handed art form and feeding times turned into opportunities for closeness and bonding. Each day brought on new discoveries, not just about my child, but about myself.

My mother struggled to understand my insistence on doing things myself. I saw the worry in her eyes and the desire to step in and help, but I needed her to understand that this wasn't about rejecting her support. I wanted to embrace my journey and fully inhabit my role as a mother. As the weeks turned into months and my son grew, I found myself growing too. My confidence as a mother blossomed and the fears and doubts that had plagued me early on began to fade and were replaced by a deep-seated belief in my abilities.

I realize now that those early days of motherhood were about more than just caring for my child. I was actively reclaiming parts of myself I thought I had lost in the accident and redefining what was possible. I was finally pushing beyond the limitations that others, and sometimes myself, had assigned me.

I've always been wary of nannies and outside help. It's not that I don't appreciate the concept or understand why others might need it, but I had fought so hard for my independence that the idea of handing over any part of my parental responsibilities felt like a step backward.

The instinct to be hands-on has served me well in many ways, particularly when it came to healthcare for my children. I developed a keen sense of when to take action and how to be there for them in those crucial moments. It's as if my own experiences with hospitals and recovery have honed a sixth sense for my kids' wellbeing.

I was once offered the prestigious opportunity to speak at a conference, the Africa America Institute's Annual State of Africa conference, that could have opened doors for my career. But, as the date approached, I felt an undeniable unease about leaving my child with our relatively new nanny. The thought of entrusting my little one to someone who was still essentially a stranger gnawed at me. Some might call it paranoia, but I've learned to trust these instincts because they've been hard-won through years of navigating a world that wasn't always designed for someone with my challenges. So, I made the difficult decision to decline the speaking engagement. It wasn't an easy choice but, in my heart, I knew it was the right one.

The relationship with my mother during this time was complicated. Her help, while well-intentioned, often felt more like teaching than guiding. There was always an underlying current of, "This is how it should be done," rather than, "How can I support you in doing this your way?"

I found myself conflicted about accepting her offers of help—not because I didn't appreciate the support, but because it often felt accompanied by unspoken expectations. It had to be done her way or no way at all. This approach created unnecessary tension between us, a push and pull that added stress to an already challenging situation. I couldn't help but reflect on the irony. I was a woman who had overcome so much, who had pushed against societal expectations and limitations, yet I was struggling to assert my autonomy in my own home and with my own children.

When we returned to Ghana from the States, my mother stayed to help for two weeks. Those fourteen days were a mixed bag of gratitude and frustration. I appreciated her presence, the extra set of hands, and the wealth of knowledge she brought, but I was also counting down the days until I could fully embrace my role as a mother without her hovering presence. As those two weeks came to an end, I felt a mix of emotions.

There was relief at the thought of finally being able to parent on my own terms, but there was also a tinge of sadness. I hoped that our relationship could be different and that we could find a way to work together without the underlying tension. More than anything, I felt a renewed determination. As I watched my mother leave, I made a silent promise to myself and to my children that I would be the mother I needed to be, not the one others expected me to be. I would find my own way by drawing on the strength and resilience that had carried me through so much already.

In the quiet of that moment, I held my child close and realized that this, too, was part of my journey. Learning how to be a mother, to trust my instincts, and to balance independence with the need for support were all part of the ongoing process of discovering who I was meant to be.

In the intricate dance of family life, I've always prided myself on being there for my children. I give them my all and would have given them 200% if such a thing were possible. Commitment comes from a deep well of love and a place of fierce determination. Having fought so hard for my independence and for the right to be a mother despite my disability, I poured every ounce of energy into this role, but this dedication has not been without its costs. Andy, the father of my children, often felt sidelined.

"You don't prioritize me," he'd say, his voice tinged with hurt and frustration. "We should come first." His words would hang in the air between us as a stark reminder of the delicate balance I was failing to strike.

I couldn't deny the truth in his words, yet I struggled to change. Everything I do, every decision I make, is with my children in mind. My disability has heightened my sense of responsibility and drives me to prove to the world, and to myself, that I can be an exceptional mother despite the challenges I've faced.

The journey of parenting as a person with a disability is fraught with frustrations. Simple tasks that others take for granted can become monumental challenges. Yet, despite the difficulties and the exhaustion that seeps into my bones at the end of each day, I wouldn't have it any other way. I'd rather go through this process directly with my kids and experience every high and low than step back and let others take the reins.

There's a bittersweet irony in the fact that I am the sole custodian on my children's US birth certificates. The authorities wouldn't allow Andy's name to be included and this bureaucratic decision fails to reflect the reality of our family life. It's a reminder of the hurdles we face and how our family doesn't fit neatly into predetermined boxes.

I've always been quick to anger. My temper flares hot and fast. It's a trait I'm not proud of, and one that I've

struggled to control, but motherhood has been a transformative experience in more ways than one. Having
children has smoothed my rough edges and made me
more even-keeled. The responsibility of shaping young
lives and being a role model for my children has forced
me to confront this aspect of myself. Now, when I feel
that familiar heat of anger rising, I take a deep breath
and picture my children's faces, their trusting eyes
looking up at me. It's not always easy, and I'm far from
perfect, but I'm learning. I'm growing alongside my children and their presence in my life pushes me to be a
better version of myself.

This journey of motherhood, with all its joys and
challenges, has become the most profound chapter of
my life story. It's a daily lesson in patience, love, and the
power of perseverance. Each day brings new challenges
and new opportunities for growth.

As I navigate this path, I'm acutely aware of the
example I'm setting for my children. They're watching
me overcome obstacles, adapt to challenges, and push
through frustrations. Yes, my dedication to my children
may sometimes overshadow other aspects of my life and
there are days when the weight of responsibility feels
overwhelming but, in those moments, I remind myself
of how far I've come and of the odds I've defied to be
with my children.

My mother, despite her role as a grandmother, carries

herself with the energy of a much younger woman. Her Ghanaian upbringing granted her a vibrant social life that defies age. When she visits my home, she's a whirlwind of activity. She constantly juggles two phones—one buzzing incessantly while she chats away on the other. Her social network is a vast and varied tapestry woven from high school friends, church acquaintances, and community connections.

This social butterfly also wears the hat of a businesswoman who manages a guesthouse complete with a restaurant and bar. It's a family venture, one we all invested in together. We bought the land, built the property from the ground up, and poured our hopes and dreams into its foundations. But, like many family businesses, it became entangled in personal drama when my father decided to leave us for a new family. With cold precision, he extracted his investment down to the last dollar and left behind a void that echoed with more than just financial loss. The business, Lizgat Company Limited, operates under the name Lizgat Hotel. It's a modest 12-room guesthouse with a restaurant and bar nestled at the back. We've also expanded to include a fuel station with a minimart to diversify our interests in the local economy. My sister remains an owner in name only. She is a silent partner in a venture that has become a symbol of our family's resilience and adaptability.

The origins of this business trace back to 2006, a

pivotal year when we moved back to Ghana for my traditional treatment. My father, still part of our family unit then, spearheaded the construction. It was a time of hope and new beginnings tinged with the uncertainty of my health struggles. Little did we know then how this property would become a lifeline and a potential safety net in times of need.

There's a certain security in knowing that, if push came to shove, we could sell the property and I'd be set for life. It's not something I dwell on often but, in moments of quiet reflection, I'm grateful for this backup plan. It's a stark contrast to the financial insecurity that many in my position face. This financial cushion, however, has led to some uncomfortable situations. I can't count the number of times I've been asked, by dates and acquaintances alike, if I received a settlement from my accident. The question always catches me off guard. It's a reminder of how people view disability through a lens of compensation and monetary value as if they're trying to quantify my struggle and put a price tag on my experiences.

Junior, a ghost from my past, made an unexpected reappearance in my life. His request, "Can you help me get to the US?" was as blunt as it was predictable.

Managing family businesses, navigating complex relationships, and dealing with presumptions about my financial status are all part of the intricate tapestry of my life post-accident. With each installment in this story, I am learning more about resilience, adaptation, and how to navigate a world that often doesn't know how to categorize or understand me.

The guesthouse has become a symbol of our ability to build something lasting, even in the face of personal upheaval. As I watch guests come and go and oversee the day-to-day operations at times alongside my mother, I'm reminded that life, like this business, is about adapting, growing, and finding strength in the most unexpected places.

## CHAPTER 9

# Hearts in Transit

WHEN I WAS FIVE YEARS OLD, my father embarked on a journey that would shape our family's future. He left for Holland, chasing work opportunities that promised a better life for us all. Those five years of his absence felt like an eternity to my young self. He left a gaping hole in our family unit that nothing could quite fill. I was ten by the time he returned and it coincided with an unexpected stroke of luck—my mother had won the US visa lottery. This convergence of events felt like fate, as if a new chapter opened for our family just as another was closing.

During those early years, my relationship with my father was something I treasured deeply. In a culture where traditional gender roles often dictated family dynamics, my father defied expectations. He was the one who would patiently do my sister's hair and mine and his large hands were surprisingly gentle as they worked through our tangles. The kitchen was his domain too and he often filled our home with the aromatic scents of his cooking. These memories of my father—his presence, his care, and his involvement in the minutiae of our daily lives—were much different than my recollections of my mother during that time. It's not that she was absent, not physically at least, but her presence was different. Always busy and always involved in something beyond the immediate confines of our home.

I remember her as a whirlwind of activity. She constantly moved between work, church commitments, and social engagements. Her energy was admirable and her dedication to her various roles was evident but, as a child, I found it hard to connect with the ever-moving force that was my mother. Only now can I appreciate the complexity of the situation. My mother was likely doing what she thought was best for our family—working hard to provide, staying involved in the community, and setting an example of an active, engaged life—but, to my younger self, it felt like she was always just out of reach.

My father's nurturing presence and my mother's more distant energy shaped my understanding of family and parental roles in ways I'm still unpacking today. It has influenced how I view my own role as a parent and forces me to strive for a balance between providing for my children and being present in their daily lives. I find myself wondering how different things might have been if the roles had been reversed; if it had been my mother who stayed home while my father worked long hours and engaged in community activities. Would I have felt the same connection to her that I did to my father? Would my understanding of motherhood be fundamentally different?

These questions linger, not as regrets or criticisms, but as reflections on the complex tapestry of family life. They remind me that our childhood experiences shape us in profound ways and influence our perceptions and behaviors long into adulthood. As I navigate my own journey as a parent, I often find myself drawing on these early experiences. I strive to emulate my father's hands-on approach and his willingness to engage in the everyday tasks of childcare regardless of traditional gender expectations. At the same time, I've gained a new appreciation for my mother's dedication to her work and community and now understand the sacrifices and difficult choices that come with balancing family and outside commitments. The lessons I've taken from both my parents have blended to form my own unique approach to parenting. It's an approach that values presence and engagement and seeks to balance the need to provide with the desire to be deeply involved in my children's daily lives. This approach recognizes the complexities of family life and how our roles and relationships evolve over time.

As THE YEARS WENT BY, my understanding of the complex dynamics that shaped our family grew. My mother, despite her seemingly distant presence in my childhood, emerged as the financial linchpin of our household. Her hard work and dedication ensured that we were never without a steady foundation beneath our feet. This realization was a testament to the often unseen sacrifices parents make for their children. It was even later that I discovered a truth about my father that cast our relationship in a new light. He had always wanted a son. This desire, deeply rooted and unspoken, had heavily influenced his interactions with us. The knowledge that he sought out a second marriage to fulfill the dream of having sons was a difficult pill to swallow. He has two sons; however, the irony wasn't lost on me when I learned he now has twin girls from this new relationship.

Looking back, I could see how this unfulfilled wish had colored our upbringing. My father had raised us with a touch of masculinity and encouraged interests that might traditionally be considered more suited to boys. Sports became a focal point and a shared language between us in an attempt to bridge the gap between the daughters he had and the son he'd longed for. I often find myself questioning how much of my own identity has been shaped by this unspoken desire. Had I embraced certain interests and certain ways of being in an unconscious effort to be the child my father wanted? The line between my authentic self and the one molded by my father's expectations is now blurred.

As I delved deeper into understanding my father, I learned that his own childhood was marked by the absence of a father figure. It was a missing piece of the puzzle and helped to explain his intense desire for a son. He wanted to create the father-son bond he had never experienced to fill a void of his own.

But this pain and longing didn't always manifest in healthy ways. While never physically abusive, my father's frustration often came out as verbal outbursts. "Dad's angry again!" became a familiar refrain in our household. His anger, I now realize, was a complex mix of disappointment, unfulfilled dreams, and perhaps a touch of guilt for feeling that disappointment in the first place. Living with this undercurrent of anger was challenging. It created a tense atmosphere where walking on eggshells was necessary to avoid flipping whatever switch would trigger the next outburst. As children, we learned to navigate these emotional minefields and developed a keen sense of our father's moods and the invisible lines we shouldn't cross.

Yet, despite the challenges, there was love. It was a complicated love that was tangled up with expectations and unspoken desires, but it was love, nonetheless. My father's efforts to connect with us through sports, his gentle hands braiding our hair, or his presence in the kitchen were all expressions of love, however imperfect. These aspects of my childhood highlight the complexity of family relationships.

My dad also worked outside the home and, at one point, earned more than my mother. But somehow, he seemed better able to balance work and his domestic role at home, defying typical gender norms. The interplay between my mother's perceived financial stability and my father's emotional turbulence, the push and pull of expectations versus reality, and the ways that our parents' unfulfilled dreams shape our own lives is a tapestry of human experience that continues to influence me today.

I find myself hyper-aware of the unspoken messages I might be sending to my children. I strive to love them for who they are, not for who I might wish them to be, but I also recognize the inevitability of our own experiences coloring our parenting and how our past invariably shapes our present. These realizations don't negate the love I feel for my parents or the appreciation I have for the sacrifices they made. Instead, they add depth to my understanding of them as complex, flawed human beings who did their best with the tools they had. It's a perspective that brings compassion, both for them and for myself, as I navigate my own path through parenthood.

I sometimes hear my children's voices ringing in my ears, "You're always yelling, Mom!" Their words hit me like a punch to the gut and are a stark reminder of a cycle that I've been desperately trying to break. My dad's temper, while never manifesting in physical abuse, cast a long shadow over our family life. Now, as a parent myself, I find echoes of his anger in my own voice and it terrifies me. Am I becoming the very thing I promised myself I'd never be?

This struggle with anger, an inherited trait I'm fighting against, has created an imbalance in my relationship with my children. Too often, I find myself falling back on an authoritarian stance. It's a posturing that feels foreign to me, yet I slip into it in moments of frustration. Each time it happens, I'm reminded of the power dynamics I witnessed growing up and the unequal footing that characterized my relationship with my father.

The complexity of these family dynamics was never more apparent than on the day my sister and I graduated. By some twist of fate or poor planning, our ceremonies were scheduled for the same day and forced our parents to make an impossible choice. They decided to split up and each attended one ceremony. I remember the anticipation I felt, knowing my mother would be in the audience as I walked across the stage, but it was tempered by a gnawing disappointment that my father wouldn't be there to see this milestone.

When my father returned from my sister's graduation, his words cut deep.

"I'm so disappointed," he said, and, though he didn't elaborate, the implication hung heavy in the air. Was he disappointed in missing my ceremony? In attending my sister's instead? Or was it something else entirely? The ambiguity of his statement left room for all my insecurities to flourish. This moment encapsulated the unspoken expectations, the constant sense of falling short, and the struggle for attention and approval in my family.

Our parents' choices, however well-intentioned, can leave lasting impacts on their children. We inherit an intricate web of emotions and behaviors from our parents. The anger I'm fighting against and the authoritarian tendencies I'm trying to curb are not just personal flaws, but the remnants of a legacy I'm still grappling with.

Yet, in acknowledging these struggles, I also see an opportunity for growth and change. Each time I catch myself raising my voice or am tempted to fall back on "because I said so" parenting, I give myself a choice. I can either perpetuate the cycle or I can pause, take a breath, and choose a different path. It's not easy, breaking generational patterns never is, but when I manage to respond with patience instead of anger or I listen to my children instead of demanding blind obedience, I feel a small victory. It's in these moments that I'm not just parenting my children, but also healing the wounded child within myself.

The journey is ongoing and filled with missteps and moments of doubt, but, as I continue to navigate this path, I hold onto the hope that my children will remember not only the times I yelled, but also the times I apologized and the times I tried to do better. I also hold onto the hope that, in witnessing my struggle to break this cycle, they, too, will be empowered to forge healthier relationships in their own lives.

The complexities of family relationships have always been a central theme in my life. Each connection contributes to a tapestry of love, resentment, and unspoken expectations. My relationship with my mother, in particular, has been a source of both comfort and conflict. For as long as I can remember, there's been an unspoken favoritism towards my sister — a subtle yet unmistakable preference that has colored our family dynamics. This favoritism manifested in small ways. She always received a softer tone of voice, a more indulgent smile, and a quicker rush to defend. It wasn't something we ever discussed openly, but it was there as an invisible current shaping the flow of our family life. As a child, I couldn't articulate why it hurt so much. As an adult, I struggle with the lingering effects of feeling second-best in my mother's eyes.

My relationship with my sister, on the other hand, is a study in contrasts. There's a bond there that has been forged in shared experiences and the unique understanding that only siblings can have. I remember the day she got her nose ring—a small act of rebellion that seemed to symbolize the growing differences between us. I admired her courage, even as I felt a twinge of envy at her boldness.

Before the accident, my sister and I were inseparable. Growing up in Ghana, we moved through life in tandem. We attended the same schools, went to the same birthday parties, and shared the same circle of friends. We were two parts of a whole and our identities were so intertwined that it was sometimes hard to know where one ended and the other began until, suddenly, our paths diverged. My accident created both a physical and emotional divide between my sister and me. While she continued on the trajectory we had both been on, I found myself navigating a new reality that was defined by challenges and limitations I had never anticipated. This divergence added a layer of complexity to our relationship, a mix of deep love and unspoken resentment, that we're still learning to navigate.

Now, my relationship with my father is defined more by absence than presence. He is a void that aches with the memory of what once was. Despite the current estrangement, I find myself yearning for a partner, a father figure for my own children, who embodies the best of what he was. It's a paradox I'm still trying to reconcile. How can I long for someone like him in my life when he has chosen to remove himself from it?

I don't understand his decision to step away. It's a question that haunts me in quiet moments, like a puzzle I can't seem to solve. Was it the pressure of dealing with my disability? The strain of watching his daughter's life take such an unexpected turn was simply too much to handle. Or was it something deeper, a flaw in our relationship that had always been there, just waiting for the right moment to fracture completely? His new wife, younger than me, is a figure I regard with a strange detachment. I harbor no particular feelings towards her. She's a stranger who has stepped into a role in my father's life that I no longer have access to. Sometimes I wonder if she knows about the daughters her husband left behind. Does she ever think about the stepdaughters she's never met? These relationships—with my mother, my sister, my father—form the cornerstone of my identity. They're the foundation upon which I've built my understanding of love, family, and belonging. Even in their imperfections, the hurt and confusion they sometimes bring, they've shaped me into who I am.

As I navigate my own journey as a parent, I find myself constantly referring to these relationships and using them as both a guide and a cautionary tale. I strive to love my children equally; to be present in their lives in a way my father is not in mine, and to foster a bond between them that can weather any storm. It's not always easy. The echoes of my past often resurface in unexpected ways. But, in acknowledging these influences and consciously choosing which patterns to perpetuate and which to break, I'm not just parenting my children. I'm also "parenting" myself, healing old wounds, and creating a new narrative of what family can be.

In the end, isn't that what we're all trying to do? We all take the lessons from our past, both good and bad, and use them to create a better future. This process of understanding and reconciling our family relationships is a journey without end but, in this journey, we find our truest selves.

CHAPTER 10

# The Space Between Here and There

THERE'S A PECULIAR KIND OF LONELINESS that comes with belonging nowhere and everywhere at once. After a decade of traversing between the United States and Ghana, I've come to realize that I don't truly belong in either place. It's a realization that settles in your bones and becomes part of your DNA, as natural as breathing yet just as unconscious until something forces you to notice it.

In Ghana, I am forever marked as "the American." The label comes with a weight of expectations and assumptions that I never asked to carry. Meanwhile, in the United States, I navigate a complex web of identities—a woman, a person of color, an individual with a disability—each one adding another layer to the already intricate dance of belonging. But perhaps the most profound identity I wrestle with is that of being a foreigner in my own ancestral land.

The irony doesn't escape me. In Ghana, my disability has become more pronounced, not just physically but socially. I encounter buildings without elevators or ramps, and government offices as inaccessible today as they were a decade ago. People stare—not the quick, furtive glances I've grown accustomed to in the States, but long, unabashed looks that make me acutely aware of my difference. Here, my limitations are not just physical barriers to overcome; they become social walls that separate me from fully integrating into the society I supposedly belong to.

My children's experiences add another layer of complexity to this cultural tightrope walk. Their American citizenship wasn't left to chance like mine, which came through the visa lottery. For them, it was a deliberate choice, a calculated decision to provide them with opportunities I could only dream of. Yet watching them navigate between these worlds brings its own kind of heartache. Their accents shift like chameleons—more American after time in the States, gradually fading back to Ghanaian rhythms upon return. Each transformation is met with subtle judgments: the underlying assumption that sounding American is somehow "better," more sophisticated, while their Ghanaian cadence is viewed as something to be overcome.

The truth is, I've never wanted to fully embrace either identity at the expense of the other. To become completely American would mean losing essential parts of myself, while fully embodying my Ghanaian identity feels impossible after years of cultural adaptation. Instead, I exist in this liminal space, this in-between world where belonging is more about creating your own space than fitting into pre-existing ones.

This duality becomes most apparent in my professional life. At meetings and events in Ghana, I often find myself overlooked despite my credentials—two degrees, years of experience, and a track record of accomplishments that should speak for themselves. Sometimes I wonder if it's my disability that causes others to take me less seriously, or if it's the complex intersection of being a woman, being perceived as foreign, and having physical limitations. The subtle dismissals come in many forms: being passed over in discussions, having my contributions minimized, or simply being treated as if my presence is somehow less valid than others.

I remember my time as a Vlisco brand ambassador, standing among other accomplished women, all of us equally capable and intelligent. Yet there was always that undercurrent, that subtle difference in how people engaged with me compared to the others. It wasn't overt discrimination—those kinds of battles I've learned to fight. Instead, it was the kind of gentle dismissal that's harder to challenge, the type that makes you question whether you're imagining things.

The social stigma in Ghana carries a different weight than in the United States. When I was pregnant, my own aunts questioned whether I could have a natural birth, their doubt masquerading as concern. Dating becomes a complex maze of others' preconceptions about what someone with a disability can or cannot do. I think of my friend's daughter, twenty years old and autistic, whose mother worries endlessly about her chances for a normal life, for romance, for all the experiences that others take for granted. These concerns might exist elsewhere, but here they become barriers, unspoken rules about who gets to live a full life.

The daily rhythms of life in Ghana present their own unique challenges. Without our nanny, mornings are particularly hectic as I navigate getting the kids ready for school. It's these everyday moments that highlight the intricate dance of independence and interdependence that defines my life here. Each small task becomes a testament to resilience, a quiet rebellion against the limitations others might see in me.

In the United States, my disability often feels like just one part of who I am. Here, it becomes a lens through which every aspect of my life is viewed and judged. Yet this is home too—complicated, challenging, but still mine. It's where my children are growing up, where I've built my organization, where I continue to fight for the rights and dignity of others facing similar battles.

My advocacy work in Ghana has become a bridge between these two worlds I inhabit. When I lobby for students with dyslexia or dyscalculia to receive proper accommodations in school, I bring my American experience of disability rights to bear on Ghanaian institutional structures. I remember one student, in particular, dismissed by her teachers as lazy and stupid until we fought for proper testing and accommodations. It took my physical presence in the school head's office, explaining the nature of learning disabilities, to shift the narrative from blame to support.

These moments of advocacy reveal both the challenge and the opportunity of straddling two cultures. My American education and exposure to disability rights give me the language and framework to fight for change, while my Ghanaian identity provides the cultural understanding needed to make that change effective. When I speak to school administrators or government officials, I must carefully balance Western concepts of accessibility and accommodation with local cultural perspectives.

Sometimes, this cultural translation feels like walking a tightrope. I find myself code-switching not just in language but in entire worldviews. In meetings with international donors, I speak the language of human rights and educational access. With local officials, I might frame the same concepts in terms of community support and family values. Each interaction requires a careful calibration of which parts of my identity to emphasize and which to softly background.

The girls in our program, The Girls Education Initiative Ghana, often face similar challenges of identity and belonging, though in different ways. Many come from backgrounds where disability or learning differences are seen as spiritual problems rather than educational challenges. Our work isn't just about providing academic support; it's about helping these young women navigate the complex intersection of traditional beliefs and modern educational practices.

When I look at my own children, I see them developing their own form of cultural agility. They switch effortlessly between worlds, their identities as fluid as their accents. Yet I worry about the weight of this inheritance—this need to constantly navigate between cultures, to belong everywhere and nowhere at once. Will they see it as a burden or a gift? Will they understand that their American citizenship, while deliberately chosen, doesn't have to define them any more than their Ghanaian heritage does?

The longer I walk this path between cultures, the more I understand that true belonging isn't about fitting perfectly into any one world. It's about creating your own space, one that accommodates all the complexities of who you are. When people ask me if I feel more American or more Ghanaian, I've learned to embrace the ambiguity of my answer: I am both, and perhaps neither, and that's perfectly fine.

I think about my work here in Ghana, and how my organization has evolved over the past decade. Every small victory—every girl who receives proper educational accommodations, every mind we open to new possibilities—represents a blend of both worlds. We take what works from each culture: the emphasis on individual rights and accommodation from the West, and the strong sense of community and family support from Ghana.

The physical barriers I face daily in Ghana—the lack of elevators, and the inaccessible buildings—remind me that change is still needed. But they also remind me why I chose to base myself here, where the challenges are greater but so is the potential for impact. In the United States, I might find more physical accessibility, but here I can help shape the future of accessibility for generations to come.

My children are growing up in this in-between space, learning to navigate multiple identities just as I have. I watch them move seamlessly between cultures, switching languages and mannerisms with an ease I sometimes envy. They're creating their own version of belonging, one that doesn't require choosing between worlds but embraces the richness of both.

Perhaps that's the greatest lesson in all of this: belonging isn't about finding a perfect fit in any one place. It's about learning to carry your home within you, about creating spaces where others like you can find their own way of belonging. As I continue to build bridges between these worlds—through my organization, through my advocacy, and through my daily life—I'm no longer searching for where I belong. Instead, I'm creating a new kind of belonging, one that makes room for all the complexities and contradictions of who I am.

In the end, it's not about being American enough or Ghanaian enough. It's about being exactly who I am—a woman who has learned to turn the challenge of existing between worlds into a strength, a mother who is teaching her children to do the same, and an advocate who understands that real change often comes from those who can see beyond the boundaries of any one culture.

# CHAPTER 11

# Forward Motion

As I DUG DEEPER, trying to unravel the mystery of this child's struggles, I stumbled upon a harsh reality that shook me to my core. In this part of the world, having a disability often meant being rendered invisible. The concept was so foreign to me, so at odds with everything I had fought for in my own life, that it took my breath away.

I learned that children with disabilities were often segregated into special schools or institutions that promised resources but often delivered isolation. For those from poor families, the outlook was even bleaker. Their chances of receiving a quality education, and of living a life comparable to their peers, were slim at best.

This realization hit me like a physical blow. Here I was, a woman who had fought tooth and nail for my education, who had pushed against the boundaries of what society deemed possible for someone with a disability. And yet, in another part of the world, children like me were being written off before they even had a chance to begin.

The injustice of it all ignited a fire within me. I thought of my own journey, the opportunities I had been given, and the obstacles I had overcome. How different would my life have been if I had been born into a society that viewed my disability as a reason to hide me away?

As I continued my research, each new piece of information felt like a puzzle piece falling into place. The picture it revealed was one of systemic inequality, of societal norms that perpetuated discrimination under the guise of protection. It was a vicious cycle—lack of education led to lack of opportunity, which in turn reinforced the belief that those with disabilities had nothing to contribute to society.

But amidst this grim reality, I also found hope. I met educators and advocates who were fighting to change the narrative and create inclusive environments where all children could learn and thrive. Their passion was contagious, and I found myself drawn into their cause.

This experience in Ghana, coupled with my studies at Wagner, began to shape my understanding of disability rights on a global scale. It wasn't just about accessibility ramps or special education programs. It was about changing mindsets, challenging deeply ingrained societal norms, and fighting for the basic human right to be seen, heard, and valued.

As I delved deeper into this work, I couldn't help but draw parallels to my own life. How many times had I been underestimated, written off, or deemed incapable? How often have I had to prove my worth in a world that wasn't designed for people like me?

These questions fueled my research, driving me to explore the intersections of disability, poverty, and education. I began to see my own experiences not just as personal challenges, but as part of a larger narrative of disability rights and social justice.

The girl in that first-grade classroom in Ghana had unknowingly set me on a path that would define my academic and professional future. Her struggles became a catalyst for my own growth, pushing me to look beyond my personal experiences and engage with the global realities of living with a disability.

As I continued my studies at Wagner, this newfound passion infused everything I did. Each class and project became an opportunity to explore these issues further and challenge my own assumptions and those of my peers. I was no longer just studying public administration and nonprofit management—I was on a mission to understand and change the systems that perpetuated inequality.

Looking back, I realize that being waitlisted by NYU Wagner was perhaps one of the best things that could have happened to me. It led me to Ghana and eventually South Africa, and ultimately to a deeper understanding of my place in the world and the change I wanted to create.

The journey ahead would be challenging, I knew. Changing deeply ingrained societal norms and systems is never easy. But as I thought of that young girl in Ghana, of all the children like her around the world, I knew that this was a fight worth having. And I was ready to take it on, armed with my education, my experiences, and an unwavering belief in the potential of every individual, regardless of their abilities or disabilities.

IN THE BUSTLING CLASSROOMS of Ghana and South Africa, where I went to do graduate research on inclusive education policies in classrooms, two girls stood out from the rest. There was Lungile, in South Africa, who was both deaf and mute, her silence spoke volumes in a world that often overlooked those who couldn't shout to be heard. Something about her drew me in, a magnetic pull I couldn't explain until the realization hit—I saw myself in her. Then there was Priscilla, in Ghana, who I met while getting traditional treatments in Ghana in 2006.

Me and Lungile in South Africa.

Her struggles to communicate, to be understood, to simply exist in a world not designed for her needs, transported me back to those difficult days after my accident. The frustration of trying to make myself understood when words failed me, the isolation of being trapped in a body that no longer functioned as it once had—all these memories came flooding back. In her determined eyes, I saw the same resilience that had pulled me through those dark times.

Time spent with these young disabled girls became a journey of self-reflection. The girl with the limp who moved with a determination that belied her physical challenges reminded me of my own stubborn refusal to be defined by my disability. Another struggled with tasks requiring fine motor skills, her frustration evident as she tried again and again, just as I had done during my rehabilitation.

Each of these girls carried a piece of my story, a fragment of the journey I had traveled. Their challenges were different, yet so familiar. Their struggles resonated with me on a level I hadn't experienced before. It was as if the universe was holding up a mirror, showing me not just who I had been, but who I could be for these girls.

Nearing the end of my graduate studies, a clarity I had never known before washed over me. This was it. This was what I was meant to do. All the twists and turns of my life —the accident, the recovery, the struggles, and the triumphs—had led me to this moment, this realization. My purpose became clear: to work with these girls, to be the advocate and support I wished I had.

In 2013, with my graduate degree in hand and a fire in my heart, I returned to Ghana to register my organization. The decision to base myself there wasn't just about the work—it was about self-preservation. Ghana, with its laid-back atmosphere and slower rhythm, offered exactly what I needed. It was a place where I could focus on my mission without constantly fighting against the current of a fast-paced society. The irony wasn't lost on me—I had come full circle, returning to the country of my roots to plant the seeds of change.

Navigating the bureaucratic maze of registering a non-profit led to reflection on the journey that had brought me here. From the scared, confused girl lying in a hospital bed to the determined woman filling out paperwork to start an organization—it felt like a lifetime had passed, and in many ways, it had.

The challenges ahead were daunting. Changing perceptions about disability, especially in a society where such issues were often hidden away, would be an uphill battle. But thoughts of the girls I had met, of their potential and their dreams, fueled my determination. This was a fight worth having.

Every form filled out, and every official met with, was a step towards creating a world where girls like the ones I had met could thrive. A world where disability didn't mean invisibility, where different abilities were celebrated rather than hidden away.

Settling into my new life in Ghana brought a sense of purpose I had never known before. The girl who had once faced exorcism attempts was now starting a revolution of her own—a quiet one, perhaps, but no less powerful for its subtlety. With each day, each small victory, I was rewriting the narrative of disability, not just for myself, but for all the girls who would come after me.

The journey of building my organization began in earnest as we started recruiting our first cohort of students. We focused on 6th and 7th graders, girls on the cusp of middle school, their futures stretching out before them like uncharted territory. Fourteen young souls joined us that first year, each with her own story, her own challenges, and her own boundless potential.

I remember looking at their faces during our first meeting, a mix of curiosity, apprehension, and hope reflected in their eyes. These girls, I realized, were entrusting us with their dreams, their aspirations. The weight of that responsibility settled on my shoulders, not as a burden, but as a calling.

Our work didn't go unnoticed. In a twist of fate that still amazes me, my story found its way into the pages of Forbes Woman Africa. Seeing my name in print, my journey laid out for all to read was a surreal experience. It wasn't about personal glory, but about the platform it provided for our cause. Each reader of that article was another potential ally in our fight for equality and inclusion.

The publication opened doors I hadn't even known existed. President Obama's initiative, aimed at bridging the gap between Africa and America, suddenly became a tangible opportunity. I was recruited for Cohort 1 of the Young African Center's Regional Leadership Conference (YALI-RLC) but joined Cohort 3 in 2016 instead. This is because, in 2015, I was the Vlisco Brand Ambassador in Ghana and the duties didn't allow for YALI-RLC participation. As an American, I was not eligible for the Mandela Washington Fellowship in D.C., which would have been an opportunity I would have loved to have received.

Being the 2015 Ghana Vlisco Brand Ambassador for the textile company in Holland, was also an amazing experience. And the symbolism was powerful. Textiles, with their interwoven threads creating beautiful patterns, mirrored the work we were doing—weaving together education, advocacy, and empowerment to create a tapestry of change.

One of the notable challenges and experiences as a brand ambassador was the fact that designers weren't used to dressing a person with a physical difference and often needed to adapt how they made my clothes. For example, my clothes had buttons and zippers in the front rather than the back to accommodate me and ensure my independence. Culturally, Ghanaian designers weren't familiar with this, and my requests at times came off as though I was making many demands.

But there I found myself, in 2016, having been selected as part of the Yali Regional Fellowship in Ghana. It was all a bit surreal—me, the girl who had once been told she might never walk again, now crossing oceans and continents as an ambassador for change.

I was dividing my time between Ghana and New York City so I could participate in the RLC as a resident of Ghana in time for it starting in 2016. The fellowship was a whirlwind of learning, networking, and growth. I soaked up every experience, every conversation, every nugget of wisdom shared. All the while, my thoughts were with the girls back home, wondering how I could translate these experiences into opportunities for them.

This role allowed me to straddle two worlds—the corporate realm, with its resources and reach, and the grassroots level where our day-to-day work took place. It was a delicate balance, but one that I embraced wholeheartedly. Every speaking engagement, every photo shoot, every meeting became an opportunity to shine a light on our cause.

As I navigated these new roles—educator, advocate, fellowship participant, brand ambassador—I often thought back to those early days of my recovery. The long hours of physical therapy, the frustration of relearning basic tasks, and the moments of despair when the future seemed impossibly bleak. How could I have known then that those challenges were preparing me for this moment?

Each girl in our program became a reminder of why this work mattered. When I saw a student master a new skill, her face lighting up with pride, I was transported back to the first time I took a step after the accident. When another girl stood up to speak, her voice shaky but determined, I remembered my own struggles to communicate during recovery.

Our work was more than just education—it was and still is about rewriting narratives, challenging assumptions, and opening doors that had long been closed. With each passing day, each small victory, we were creating ripples of change that I hoped would eventually become waves.

The path ahead was still long, the challenges numerous. But as I looked at the girls in our program, as I reflected on the opportunities that had come our way, I felt a sense of hope and determination stronger than ever before. We were not just changing lives; we were changing the very fabric of society, one thread at a time.

THE MISSION OF OUR ORGANIZATION, The Girls Education Initiative of Ghana, has always been clear: to provide academic and financial support to girls' education including applicants with special needs or disabilities. But it's more than just a mission statement for me. It's a deeply personal commitment, one that stems from my own experiences and the understanding that every girl has a unique story, a unique set of challenges, and a unique potential waiting to be unlocked.

We've made a conscious decision to stay small. It's

not about numbers or impressive statistics for us. It's about knowing each girl, understanding her story, and being able to provide the individualized support she needs. I want to be able to look into the eyes of each student and see not just a beneficiary of our program, but a young woman with dreams, fears, and the power to change her world.

This work has taken me places I never imagined I'd go. I've found myself at conferences in Kenya, sharing our experiences and learning from others doing similar work across the continent. One of the most surreal moments of this journey was speaking at the United Nations NGO Conference and subsequently the United Nations—the Commission on the Status of Women (CSW).

As our organization has grown and evolved, so too have the roles within it. I now find myself co-directing with Andy, my life partner and the longest-tenured team member in the organization. It's a complex dynamic, balancing our personal history with our professional goals, but it's a testament to our shared commitment to the cause that we've made it work.

In the early days, I was a whirlwind of activity, dropping everything at every request to speak, meet, or network. My calendar was a patchwork of commitments, each one feeling crucial to our mission. I lived and breathed the work, often at the expense of my own well-being.

But time and experience have taught me the importance of balance, of pacing myself for the long haul. I've begun the process of phasing myself out of the day-to-day operations of the organization. It's not an easy decision, but I believe it's necessary for both my personal growth and the sustainable future of our initiative.

My vision now is to move into consulting for other nonprofits. I want to take the lessons we've learned, the strategies we've developed, and use them to help other organizations maximize their impact. It's a way of multiplying our effect, of spreading the ripples of change even further.

This transition is bittersweet. Each time I step back, I feel a pang of worry. Will the girls be okay? Will the organization continue to thrive? But then I look at our team, at the capable hands I'm leaving things in, and I know it's time. Just as we encourage our girls to spread their wings and fly, I, too, must take this leap.

As I contemplate this next chapter, I'm filled with a mix of emotions. There's pride in what we've accomplished, hope for what's to come, and a touch of nostalgia for the intense, all-consuming early days of our work. But mostly, there's gratitude. Gratitude for the girls who have trusted us with their futures, for the team members who have poured their hearts into this work, and for the journey itself—every triumph, every setback, every lesson learned.

The road ahead is uncertain, but isn't that true for all of us? What I know for sure is that the spirit of our mission—to empower girls through education—will continue to guide me, whatever form my work takes. Because in the end, it's not about me or any individual. It's about creating a world where every girl, regardless of her circumstances, has the opportunity to write her own story.

And, as I prepare to turn this page in my own story, I carry with me the faces of every girl we've worked with and every life we've touched. Their strength, their resilience, their dreams—these are the things that will continue to inspire me, to drive me forward, no matter where this next chapter leads.

## CONCLUSION

# *Parting Thoughts*

As I REFLECT ON THE PAST DECADE of running my organization, and the past twenty years of my life, I'm struck by the challenges we've faced and the resilience we've shown. The struggle for funding has been constant, with only two grants won in ten years. The assumption that, as an American, I have easy access to funding couldn't be further from the truth. Our survival has depended on the generosity of individuals who know my story and believe in the power of education to transform lives.

The work has taken me to places I never imagined— from conferences in Kenya to speaking engagements at the UN. I've presented at the 2017 United Nations Commission on the Status of Women, sharing our impact and the importance of our mission. But this work, rewarding as it is, comes at a cost. Balancing the demands of the organization with my responsibilities as a mother of two has been a constant juggling act, one that often takes its toll.

As I look to the future, I find myself at a crossroads. While I hope the organization continues to thrive in the next five, ten years, I've come to terms with the possibility that it might not. I'm co-directing with Andy, my partner and the father of my children, who has been with the organization almost as long as I have. His commitment gives me hope for the organization's future, even as I consider stepping back.

Throughout this journey, my core mission has remained unchanged: to give people opportunities and to help others see individuals with disabilities in all their wholeness. My own experiences have only strengthened my resolve. The accident may have changed my physical and intellectual capabilities, but it has also given me a greater sense of purpose.

My stubborn nature, intensified by the challenges I've faced, has become one of my greatest assets. When I enter a room, I know that my limp or my arm might be the first thing people notice. But what I want them to see is my passion and my determination to achieve things that many might think impossible for someone with my physical limitations.

In spite of the aches and pains, the residual effects of the accident that I live with daily, I continue to push forward. I strive to be an example of what's possible, to challenge preconceptions about disability, and to open doors for others who might face similar obstacles.

As I close this chapter of my life and look toward the future, I'm filled with a mix of emotions. There's pride in what we've accomplished, hope for the lives we've touched, and determination to continue making a difference, whether through this organization or in new endeavors.

The journey hasn't been easy, but it has been profoundly rewarding. Each girl we've helped, each mind we've opened, each barrier we've broken down—these are the true measures of our success. And while the road ahead may be uncertain, I face it with the same stubborn determination that has brought me this far.

My story is far from over. It's a testament to the power of perseverance, the importance of education, and the limitless potential that lies within each of us, regardless of our physical abilities. As I step into the next phase of my life, I carry with me the lessons learned, the lives touched, and the unwavering belief that every individual, given the right opportunities, can defy expectations and achieve greatness.

This journey has taught me that our perceived limitations are often just that—perceptions. With determination, support, and a refusal to be defined by others' expectations, we can rewrite our own stories. And in doing so, we pave the way for others to do the same.

As I look to the future, I'm excited for the new challenges and opportunities that lie ahead. Whether I'm continuing to advocate for girls' education, consulting with other nonprofits, or embarking on an entirely new adventure, I know that the spirit of resilience and determination that has brought me this far will continue to guide me.

To every girl who has been part of our program, to every individual who has supported our mission, and to everyone who has ever felt limited by circumstances beyond their control, I say this: Your potential is limitless. Your voice matters. Your dreams are valid. And with persistence, courage, and the right support, you can overcome any obstacle and achieve things beyond your wildest imagination.

This is not the end of my story, but rather the beginning of a new chapter. And as I turn the page, I do so with gratitude for the journey that has brought me here, hope for the future that lies ahead, and an unwavering commitment to continue making a difference, one life at a time.

# Resources

National Library of Medicine, *Rehabilitation and Long-Term Care Needs After Traumatic Brain Injury*

CognitivefxUSA.com, *How to Help Someone with a Concussion or TBI*

Model Systems Knowledge Translation Center, *Staying Healthy After TBI* and *Severe Traumatic Brain Injury*

Sabinet, African Journals, *Disability and Water Taboos in Ghana: Socio-Cultural and Theological Reflections on the Environment*

Wikipedia, *Disability in Ghana*

Mayo Clinic, *Traumatic Brain Injury*

# About the Author

Elizabeth Akua-Nyarko Patterson is the founder and executive director of the Girls education initiative of Ghana, GEIG. GEIG's mission is to provide academic and financial support for girls including applicants with special needs, so they may access secondary, higher education, and professional opportunities. Since 2014 GEIG has supported students in the Ashanti and Greater Accra regions of Ghana in their transition from basic school to junior high school. Ms. Patterson holds an MPA, masters in public administration from NYU Wagner School of Public Service where she specialized in non- profit management. Ms. Patterson's research includes but not limited to Education of Marginalized People: access to education for disabled/ differently abled students in K-12 institutions in South Africa, A comparative qualitative study on single sex and co-Ed schools in New York City, Strategic Planning: City Year New York, and Performance Measurement and Management: Junior Achievement of New York, JA-New York, A more diverse Workforce: the fire department of New York City. Prior to her work with GEIG Ms. Patterson served as the Director of Communications and Marketing for The Council of Young African Leaders, CYAL and communications and marketing associate at Junior Achievement of New York, JA- New York. Ms. Patterson holds a BA in Political Science and Business.

To learn more or contact the author,
visit Eanpconsult.com

To learn more about The Girls Education Initiative:
girlsedgh.org/our-story